A JOURNEY THROUGH AMERICAN LITERATURE

A JOURNEY THROUGH AMERICAN LITERATURE

Kevin J. Hayes

OXFORD
UNIVERSITY PRESS

OXFORD

UNIVERSITY PRESS

Oxford University Press, Inc., publishes works that further
Oxford University's objective of excellence
in research, scholarship, and education.

Oxford   New York
Auckland   Cape Town   Dar es Salaam   Hong Kong   Karachi
Kuala Lumpur   Madrid   Melbourne   Mexico City   Nairobi
New Delhi   Shanghai   Taipei   Toronto

With offices in
Argentina   Austria   Brazil   Chile   Czech Republic   France   Greece
Guatemala   Hungary   Italy   Japan   Poland   Portugal   Singapore
South Korea   Switzerland   Thailand   Turkey   Ukraine   Vietnam

Published by Oxford University Press, Inc.
198 Madison Avenue, New York, NY 10016

www.oup.com

Oxford is a registered trademark of Oxford University Press

Library of Congress Cataloging-in-Publication Data
Hayes, Kevin J.
A journey through American literature / Kevin J. Hayes.
p.   cm.
Includes bibliographical references and index.
ISBN 978-0-19-986207-8 (cloth : acid-free paper) — ISBN 978-0-19-986206-1
(pbk. : acid-free paper) 1. American literature—History and criticism. I. Title.
PS121.H39   2012
810.9—dc23   2011024702

1 3 5 7 9 8 6 4 2

Printed in the United States of America
on acid-free paper

1617

For Myung-Sook

CONTENTS

LIST OF ILLUSTRATIONS

ACKNOWLEDGMENTS

During the composition of this book I had the opportunity to teach two different American literature seminars. I would like to thank the students of both courses for their lively discussions and helpful input. Many of the ideas my students and I came up with in class are incorporated here. I also kept a blog during the composition of this book, encouraging readers to respond to various questions such as what constitutes literary greatness, what are the best short stories in American literature, and what autobiographies deserve recognition as literature. I thank Rebecca Ford at Oxford University Press for overseeing my blog. And I thank everyone who responded: Mark Athitakis, Nigel Beale, Phyllis Funke, Michelle Glauser, Kelly Parisi Castro, Karen Resta, Sanjay Sipahimalani, Jerry Waxler, and Daren Young. Those respondents I know solely by their first names or initials are no less appreciated: B.D.R., Cassie, Greg, Gunter, Guy, Dave, J. D., James, Kirsty, Kristen, Maya, Rebecca, and Sharon. Jerome Loving read my manuscript thoroughly, and I am grateful for his helpful suggestions. At Oxford University

Press, I thank Shannon McLachlan for encouraging me to write this book and seeing it through the press. I also thank Christina Gibson and Brendan O'Neill for their hard work and diligence. And, as always, I thank my wife Myung-Sook for her patience, her wisdom, and her love.

A JOURNEY THROUGH AMERICAN LITERATURE

Chapter 1

Beginnings

OPENING LINES

American literature is about identity. It is about much else as well, but there may be no general theme more prevalent in it or more pertinent to it. Many American authors have made the idea of identity central to their works. Consider these famous opening lines:

My name is Arthur Gordon Pym.

Call me Ishmael.

I celebrate myself, and sing myself,

    And what I assume you shall assume,

    For every atom belonging to me as good belongs to you.

I was born a slave; but I never knew it till six years of happy childhood had passed away.

You don't know about me, without you have read a book by the name of *The Adventures of Tom Sawyer*, but that ain't no matter.

I am an invisible man.

We were somewhere around Barstow on the edge of the desert when the drugs began to take hold.

On a sticky August evening two weeks before her due date, Ashima Ganguli stands in the kitchen of a Central Square apartment, combining Rice Krispies and Planters peanuts and chopped red onion in a bowl.

The theme of personal identity links these opening lines, but by no means is this theme clear-cut or consistent from one to the next. In the first example, the opening sentence of Edgar Allan Poe's novel *The Narrative of Arthur Gordon Pym* (1838), the title character begins his personal story by introducing himself to his readers, supplying both his family name and his given name. Pym reinforces the importance of family by describing his father and grandfather. Before another chapter is through, however, he renounces home and family and stows away aboard an oceangoing vessel. His introduction suggests a stable sense of identity, yet subsequent events undercut that stability. Ensconced in the hold of the ship, Pym gets trapped in his coffin-like hideaway for so long he nearly perishes. This death-and-rebirth motif recurs frequently in American literature.

Poe was a master of the first-person point of view, which he uses in many of his most famous tales. In *The Narrative of Arthur Gordon Pym*, the first-person voice lends an immediacy to the story and blurs the distinction between author and narrator. The three-part name Poe invented for his hero resembles his own and thus reinforces the parallel. Throughout the novel, Poe continues to play with the theme of identity. Augustus, the friend who arranges for Pym to stow away, is also his doppelgänger. At times their personalities almost blend into one.

After mutiny, storm, and numerous other harrowing adventures that reduce the number of survivors aboard ship to four, Pym, Augustus, and the other two must resort to cannibalism. They choose the victim by drawing lots. Their "fearful repast" provides a literal instance of how one personality can be subsumed within another. They cut the hands, feet, and head from the body in an effort to dehumanize the victim and efface his identity, but their effort does little to minimize the horror and shame they feel.[1] This gruesome episode simultaneously shocked and intrigued twentieth-century novelist and screenwriter Terry Southern, prompting him to dub Poe "King Weirdo."[2]

Juxtaposed with the initial sentence of Poe's sailor story, the famous first sentence of *Moby-Dick* (1851) indicates the complexity of Herman Melville's style. Whereas Poe's narrator supplies his Christian name and his family name, Melville's provides only one name, which may or may not be his given name. Rather, Ishmael is what he chooses to be called. Selecting a name from the Bible, Melville's narrator creates his own identity. Like the biblical Ishmael, he, too, is an outcast and a wanderer.

Discussing the importance of revision in their preface to the screenplay for *Blood Simple* (1984), Joel and Ethan Coen assert that when Melville first composed *Moby-Dick*, he wrote, "Just call me Ishmael," but he later streamlined his prose by cancelling the

Figure 1.1 *Herman Melville*. An undated etching after a portrait by Joseph O. Eaton. Library of Congress, Prints and Photographs Division (reproduction number LC-USZ62-135949).

initial word of the sentence.[3] Though there is no evidence to support the Coen brothers' blatant assertion, it does show they recognized the familiar, conversational tone of Ishmael's opening words. Despite its rich cultural associations, Ishmael's initial sentence sounds like something one person might say upon meeting another face-to-face. Melville thus begins by establishing a rapport with his reader. Or, more precisely, he begins the narrative part of the book in an ingratiating manner. Prior to the first chapter, he presents two sections of daring front matter: "Etymology" and "Extracts." Both sections challenge readers, supplying an apparently inchoate mass of information and forcing them to make sense of it.[4] If you have made it this far, Melville essentially tells the readers of Chapter 1, then welcome.

Walt Whitman's "Song of Myself" originally appeared as part of the first edition of his defining book of verse, *Leaves of Grass* (1855). This long poem has often been called an epic, but its subject matter differs considerably from the traditional subject matter of epic verse, which usually takes nation building as its central theme. "Song of Myself" dismisses this typical subject by concentrating on the individual. Yet Whitman also makes himself a representative man, someone who stands for everyone. Perhaps Whitman's use of the individual is not so unusual for a work of American literature. In the United States, the expression of individuality *is* an expression of nationality.

Whitman's subject is apparent from his opening. The profound egotism of his first line is initially off-putting. How vain he is to talk so blatantly about himself. Of course, it is crucial to distinguish between the author and the speaker of a poem: poets can assume whatever personae they wish. Regardless, the first line still sounds self-centered. Continuing through the second line, the opening sentence seems both egotistic and antagonistic. "What I assume you shall assume"? Who is he to tell us what to assume? How dare he have the audacity to impose his assumptions on us!

The poem's third line, which concludes the opening sentence, softens Whitman's message. He reassures us that the relationship between poet and reader is a matter not of telling but of sharing. He is not imposing his assumptions on us. Rather, he is expressing his beliefs, his ideas, his feelings with the hope that we will share them. He has tremendous self-confidence and wants us to feel similarly. All men and women should celebrate themselves.

The sentence that opens "Song of Myself" sets the tone and the mood for the rest of the poem, which alternately challenges and soothes the reader. This personal epic is not just about the indi-

Figure 1.2 *Walt Whitman.* Frontispiece to Walt Whitman, *Leaves of Grass* (New York, 1855).

Figure 1.3 E. W. Kemble, *Huckleberry Finn*. Frontispiece to Mark Twain, *Adventures of Huckleberry Finn* (New York, 1885).

vidual self. Whitman—the speaker of the poem—goes out into the world, observes his fellow Americans, and chronicles their various activities. The work is filled with what have become known as Whitmanesque catalogues, long lists describing everyday people proudly living their everyday lives. "Song of Myself" is a celebration of the diversity and richness of American life. Throughout the poem Whitman continues expanding his experience. After going from the personal to the national, he proceeds to the universal.

"Song of Myself" may begin with an assertion of personal identity, but by its end the poet identifies with everyone and offers to help others who pass his way. Glossing the end of "Song of Myself," Allen Ginsberg explains that the speaker of the poem dissolves himself into the reader, making the poem a part of the reader's consciousness.[5] The three lines that close the poem may not be as well known as those that open it, but they may be more enchanting:

> Failing to fetch me at first keep encouraged,
> Missing me one place search another,
> I stop somewhere waiting for you.

Like *Narrative of the Life of Frederick Douglass* (1845), like virtually all American slave narratives, Harriet Jacobs's *Incidents in the Life of a Slave Girl* (1861) asserts the author's personal individuality in the face of the inhuman system of slavery that existed in America prior to the Civil War. Though Jacobs calls herself Linda Brent in this autobiography and also changes the names of her acquaintances, the story she tells is essentially true. The book's opening sentence suggests that despite her hatred of slavery, her personal identity is inextricably linked to her status as a slave. Furthermore, the book's opening words distinguish Jacobs from her contemporary readers, who were mostly white abolitionists. These readers could not truly understand her experience because they did not know what it was like to be born a slave. Sensitive ones could sympathize with her plight, however. Applying a famous phrase from Henry David Thoreau, Toni Morrison describes Harriet Jacobs's tone as one of "quiet desperation."[6]

Seemingly straightforward, Jacobs's first sentence is really quite sophisticated. Starting with her birth, it rushes past her early childhood, going beyond her sixth birthday to the moment she made the awful realization that she was a slave. The sentence reflects both her innocence and her experience. Written after she escaped her master, found work in New York as a nanny in Nathaniel P. Willis's family, obtained her freedom, and became active in the abolitionist movement, *Incidents* shows Jacobs's recognition that her time as a slave marked her for life.

The people Jacobs met upon escaping from slavery influenced her future and helped shape her narrative. A prominent editor and travel writer who was known as a dandified aesthete, Nathaniel P. Willis gave Jacobs one example of how to fashion a literary persona for the reading public. His sister Sarah Payson Willis, who wrote under the name Fanny Fern, gave her another. Lydia Maria Child, who established her reputation with such socially conscious historical romances as *Hobomok* (1824), undertook the task of editing Jacobs's manuscript. Despite the Willises' influence and Child's editing, Jacobs's strong-willed personality shows throughout the narrative. Her tale of endurance is an inspiring story of one woman's unflagging efforts to circumvent the control of her master and assert her humanity and personal identity.

The opening sentence of *Adventures of Huckleberry Finn* (1885) deliberately mentions *The Adventures of Tom Sawyer* (1876) even as it repudiates the earlier book. Mark Twain had written *Tom Sawyer* in the third person, assuming the persona of an outsider observing the drama of others, but he decided to write its sequel in the first person, that is, from Huck Finn's point of view. Briefly paraphrased, Huck's opening sentence says, "It does not matter whether you have read *Tom Sawyer*." But it says much more than that. Essentially, it elevates first-person narratives over third-person ones.

Like Ishmael's opening in *Moby-Dick*, Huck's first sentence has an easygoing, conversational tone. Furthermore, Huck's words establish that his identity depends on the reader's perception of him. He defines himself in negative terms. Instead of stating who he is, as Arthur Gordon Pym does, Huck acknowledges the reader's ignorance of him. Though he makes no explicit comment about his identity, his diction reveals much. In American English, few words are more telling than "ain't." Huck's use of this vulgarism brands him as uneducated and lower-class. The rest of the sentence, however, forms a counterpoint to this impression. Curious about how he has been portrayed, Huck himself has read *Tom Sawyer*. Unwilling to let that book stand as the record of his life, Huck has enough savvy to create his own self-portrait for the reading public. Instead of letting readers form an impression of him based on what Mark Twain had to say in *Tom Sawyer*, Huck prefers to tell his own story.

The simple structure of the opening sentence of Ralph Ellison's *Invisible Man* (1952) belies its complex meaning. "I am an invisible man," Ellison's narrator tells us. Unlike Arthur Gordon Pym, this narrator provides neither his family name nor his given name. Unlike Ishmael, he never even tells us what to call him. His declarative sentence destabilizes the reader. Either the first-person narrator is writing a supernatural story or he is speaking figuratively. The book's second sentence denies any supernatural associations: "No, I am not a spook like those who haunted Edgar Allan Poe." The word "spook," of course, is a double entendre. Besides referring to a ghost-like creature, the term has a history as a racial slur. In his black revolutionary novel *The Spook Who Sat by the Door* (1969), Sam Greenlee also would use the word as a double entendre, as both a racial slur and a slang term meaning a CIA agent. By saying that he is not a spook, Ellison's invisible man denies any supernatural associations and challenges all derogatory racial epithets, symbols of a demeaning identity imposed on him by others. The phrase "invisible man" basically establishes a relationship between the nameless narrator and society. He exists in a society that does not acknowledge his existence. Like General John A. B. C. Smith in Poe's short story "The Man That Was Used Up," the absence of identity paradoxically defines the invisible man.

As the prologue continues, Ellison's nameless narrator places himself with Benjamin Franklin and other figures in "the great American tradition of tinkers." In the next paragraph, he links himself to someone representing an alternative American tradition: Louis Armstrong. He also situates his own story with other major literary narratives, paralleling his underground behavior with Dante's, witnessing a black church service reminiscent of the one Ishmael attends in *Moby-Dick*, and generally comparing his experience with Dostoevsky's *Notes from the Underground* (1864), the renowned Russian novel that influenced other American literary works, including Richard Wright's short story "The Man Who Lived Underground" (1942) and Jack Kerouac's novel *The Subterraneans* (1958).

Invisible Man sustains an extraordinary level of tension. In the first chapter, for example, Ellison's title character attends a gathering of community leaders to receive a college scholarship, but he is lumped together with several other young black men and forced to engage in a brutal exhibition fight. This "battle royal" scene possesses an almost unbearable intensity, but Ellison does not let up there. The meeting between Mr. Norton, a white and wealthy college supporter, and Jim Trueblood, an incestuous black sharecropper, compels even as it repulses. The narrator's subsequent decision to take Mr. Norton to a local tavern filled with mental patients leads to an episode echoing Poe's short story "The System of Dr. Tarr and Professor Fether" (1845) and anticipating Ken Kesey's novel *One Flew over the Cuckoo's Nest* (1962). As mayhem breaks loose, the boundaries between sane and insane blur. The situation presents another take on the issue of personal identity: can people really stand apart from their social conditions?

Syntactically, the opening sentence of Hunter S. Thompson's *Fear and Loathing in Las Vegas: A Savage Journey to the Heart of the*

American Dream (1971) differs considerably from the earlier openings, yet it, too, embodies the notion of identity. Though wildly exaggerated, Thompson's book is seemingly based on his own experience. To tell the story, he adopts a fictional persona: Raoul Duke. In this regard (and maybe only in this regard), *Fear and Loathing in Las Vegas* is not dissimilar to Harriet Jacobs's *Incidents*. Both authors use a persona to mask their actual identities, to free themselves from strict adherence to truth, and to depict technically illegal behavior with impunity. Though using a fictional guise, Thompson does bear a close personal resemblance to Raoul Duke. Bill Murray, who portrayed him in the 1980 biopic *Where the Buffalo Roam*, characterized Thompson as a dangerous man "in the sense that he loves to live on the brink of excitement and the limits of human stamina and ingenuity."[7] The subject pronoun "we" in the first sentence of *Fear and Loathing in Las Vegas* refers to both Raoul Duke and Dr. Gonzo, his three-hundred-pound Samoan attorney and traveling companion, who is another personal projection.

Starting the book on the road, an east-west road, Thompson chooses a beloved American setting. The reference to Barstow, California, reinforces the road as a defining motif of American culture. "Route 66" (1946), the Bobby Troup song popularized by Nat King Cole, made that city's name familiar to millions. Situating Raoul Duke and Dr. Gonzo on the edge of the desert, Thompson reinforces the long-standing American fascination with liminal spaces, a fascination that begins with the early American frontier and extends through science fiction stories of outer space—the "final frontier," as it is called in the famous opening line from *Star Trek* (1966–69). Taking hallucinogenic drugs, Raoul Duke places himself in a liminal space in terms of personal identity as well. He conveys his willingness to put his sense of self at risk for the sake of achieving a higher consciousness. Whereas the outside world makes Ellison's narrator invisible, Raoul Duke's personal identity is clouded by drugs. Whereas the narrators of earlier American works assert their identities, Raoul Duke, embodying the tensions and uncertainties of modern American life in the 1970s, displays a willingness to escape his.

Jhumpa Lahiri's best-selling novel, *The Namesake* (2003), begins shortly before the birth of its protagonist, Gogol Ganguli. Starting the book with an image of a pregnant mother in her kitchen, Lahiri privileges the woman's traditional sphere. Having Ashima Ganguli prepare a dish made with Rice Krispies, Lahiri provides a familiar image: Rice Krispies squares are a suburban American treat familiar at bake sales and birthday parties across the country. As soon as Ashima mixes in some onion, however, we realize that she is not making a typical Rice Krispies treat. Instead, she is trying to replicate the taste of a Calcutta street food she has been craving throughout her pregnancy.

Though Ashima is doing what she can to re-create the tastes of India in her Massachusetts home, Lahiri's references to specific name brands in this novel about naming show that, try as she might, Ashima cannot escape American consumer culture. From the screens of our television, from the bold graphics of their packages, these products yell out, urging us to buy them. According to the advertising copy, Rice Krispies even talk to us: "Snap, crackle, pop!" Rice Krispies have much cultural resonance. Indeed, the product has become a symbol for the whole idea of a brand name. Commenting on his fame as a novelist, Philip Roth remarked, "To become a celebrity is to become a brand name. There is Ivory soap, Rice Krispies, and Philip Roth."[8]

As Lahiri starts *The Namesake*, she depicts Gogol Ganguli on the verge of birth amidst two contrary influences, his ethnic heritage and American consumer culture. Though brand names may shape people, they do not necessarily diminish the powerful force of personal identity, as other works of American literature suggest. Elaine Safer has observed that in Roth's 2004 novel *The Plot Against America*, Rice Krispies cereal symbolizes the Jewish mother's moral strength and goodwill.[9] And in Sam Shepard's experimental one-act play *Forensic and the Navigators* (1967), Emmet, whose appearance and initial behavior suggest a Native American heritage, refuses buckwheat pancakes, which he associates with the middle class. Instead, he demands a proletarian breakfast: "Rice Krispies and nothing else."[10] In *The Namesake*, as in Roth's novel and Shepard's play, the individual is a site of contest between family heritage and consumer culture. The strongest characters shape their identities by consciously choosing which elements they let influence their lives.

PROMOTIONAL RHETORIC

Beginning with the theme of identity, these various narratives parallel the overall history of American literature, a metanarrative that begins with the theme of identity. Even the tension between individualism and consumerism has been present from the earliest English settlements in the New World. Few genres of early American literature are more significant in terms of cultural influence than the promotional tract, meaning a work written to encourage Europeans to emigrate to America. One could say that literature and advertising have been associated since the very beginning of American literature. What the sonnet is to the literature of the English Renaissance, the promotional tract is to the literature of colonial America: a defining genre that set the tone and charted the direction the literature would take. The authors of promotional tracts describe the land, the climate, the flora, and the fauna in ways that make America as alluring as possible. While many promotional authors are overly optimistic, some paint more realistic pictures for the reader: material success is possible in the New World solely through hard work and perseverance. According to such literature, America is a land of possibility, a place where people can remake themselves, to be whoever and whatever they wish. The New World is a place to find a new identity.

Upon identifying America as a land of possibility in *Description of New England* (1616), Captain John Smith asks a rhetorical question: "Who can desire more content, that hath small means; or but only his merit to advance his fortune, than to tread, and plant that ground he hath purchased by the hazard of his life?"[11] In America, Smith asserts, success does not depend on family or fortune. Hunting, fishing, and farming provide surer ways to wealth than digging for gold. Only by working hard and taking charge of their destinies can people succeed in remaking themselves. Smith enumerates the personal characteristics of the ideal colonist: courage, dedication, diligence, honesty, industry, and judgment.

Smith's belief in the possibilities of the New World is infectious. Speaking of New England—a place name he coined—Smith observes, "And of all the four parts of the world that I have yet seene not inhabited, could I have but means to transport a Colony, I would rather live here than any where."[12] Thomas Prince, the Boston preacher who wrote *A Chronological History of New-England* (1736), a work tracing the origins of New England back to Creation, shared the sentiment: he underlined this passage in his personal copy of Smith's work.[13] Charles Olson, whose Maximus poems reflect his intimate knowledge of the New England coastline, came to Captain John Smith two centuries after Thomas Prince. Sailing along the coast after reading the *Description of New England*, Olson could feel Smith's prose come alive.[14]

Not only does promotion literature describe what the New World has to offer, it also lists what it lacks. In other words, it uses both positive and negative catalogues as rhetorical devices.[15] Smith's *Description of New England* illustrates how the negative catalogue could be used as a rhetorical device: "Here are no hard Landlords to racke us with high rents, or extorted fines to consume us, no tedious pleas in law to consume us with their many years disputations for Justice: no multitudes to occasion such impediments to good orders, as in popular States."[16]

Smith's words reveal the connection between promotion literature and the utopian impulse. As utopian authors imagined ideal places lacking the evils of contemporary society, promotional authors described real places where new societies could be established, societies free from the corruption of the Old World. America offered the opportunity of establishing a model civilization. Smith observes: "Here nature and liberty affords us that freely, which in England we want, or it costeth us dearely."[17]

In *Information to Those Who Would Remove to America* (1784), Benjamin Franklin refutes the simplistic notion that people could emigrate to America and instantly prosper. He explains: "America is the Land of Labour, and by no means what the English call *Lubberland*, and the French *Pays de Cocagne*, where the Streets are said to be pav'd with half-peck Loaves, the Houses til'd with Pancakes, and where the Fowls fly about ready roasted, crying, *Come eat me!*"[18] Like Smith's *Description of New England*, Franklin's tract excels as a promotional work because of its realistic viewpoint: it disabuses readers of whatever romantic notions they may have about America and tells them what they must really do to succeed.

Early American literature, in turn, is filled with stories of people asserting themselves, braving the environment, and enduring hardship to succeed. Toward the end of the colonial period, writers began to view the settling of America in retrospect. In *A Summary View of the Rights of British America* (1774), Thomas Jefferson shows that the early colonists had answered Captain John Smith's call

Figure 1.4 *Smith Rescued by Pocahontas*. A lithograph published by Henry Schile, 1870. Library of Congress, Prints and Photographs Division (reproduction number LC-DIG-pga-02687).

and risen to the challenge. Jefferson emphasizes how American settlers successfully planted the British colonies in North America: "Their own blood was spilt in acquiring lands for their settlement, their own fortunes expended in making that settlement effectual. For themselves they fought, for themselves they conquered, and for themselves alone they have right to hold." Self-sufficiency has long been recognized as a fundamental ideal defining the American national character. As Jefferson clarifies, self-sufficiency had become a part of the American character well before nationhood. The American colonists invested their bodies and blood in the struggle. They had earned their rights, in Jefferson's words, "at the hazard of their lives, and loss of their fortunes."[19]

Crèvecoeur's *Letters from an American Farmer* (1782), an often dazzling but occasionally disturbing account of the settler's place in the New World, incorporates much promotional rhetoric. For instance, in Letter 3, "What Is an American?" Crèvecoeur uses a negative catalogue to describe the social environs: "Here are no aristocratical families, no courts, no kings, no bishops, no ecclesiastical dominion, no invisible power giving to a few a very visible one, no great manufactures employing thousands, no great refinements of luxury."[20] Like Smith's *Description* and Franklin's *Information*, Crèvecoeur's *Letters* describes how a person can succeed in America. Crèvecoeur also attempts to define the "American." His keen intuition prompted him to draft a definition that holds up today as a kind of national ideal: "The American is a new man, who acts upon new principles; he must therefore entertain new ideas and form new opinions. From involuntary idleness, servile dependence, penury, and useless labour, he has passed to toils of a very different nature, rewarded by ample subsistence. This is an American."[21]

THE AMERICAN DREAM

Though cultural aspects of the American dream are nascent in the colonial promotion literature, the phrase "American dream" did not enter the vernacular until the early twentieth century. The notion of striving toward prosperity and personal satisfaction drives much American literature. David Graham Phillips's novel *The Husband's Story* (1911) may mark the earliest appearance of this fabled phrase in American literature. Phillips reused the phrase in *Susan Lenox: Her Fall and Rise* (1917), having his title character read novels and magazines to prepare herself "for the possible rise of fortune that is the universal American dream and hope."[22]

Before the phrase "American dream" began being used, however, the ideas it represented were codified in numerous literary works, from Benjamin Franklin's *Autobiography* (written 1771–90) to Horatio Alger's series of popular boys' books. In *The Erie Train Boy* (1890), Alger tells the story of Fred Fenton, a teenage boy working as a vendor on passenger trains crisscrossing upstate New York who is "prompt, self-reliant and possessed of unusual good sense."[23] Fred's discovery of stolen bonds reveals his ingenuity and determination, personal characteristics that lead to his social and professional success.

In terms of theme and structure, one Alger novel is pretty much the same as another, but *The Erie Train Boy* possesses documentary value for its depiction of railroad culture. The text's playfulness gives it additional interest. The pleasant young woman Fred meets on the train is named Isabel Archer. Alger lifted the character straight from Henry James's *Portrait of a Lady* (1881). Alger's clever use of James's character embodies an intertextuality that would not become prevalent in American literature until another half century passed.

Alger himself has become closely identified with the idea of the American dream. Ralph Ellison mentions him in *The Invisible Man* as he portrays wealthy college alumni returning to campus and speaking to its student body. The narrator observes: "Here upon this stage the black rite of Horatio Alger was performed to God's own acting script, with millionaires come down to portray themselves; not merely acting out the myth of their goodness, and wealth and success and power and benevolence and authority in cardboard masks, but themselves, these virtues concretely!" *Fear and Loathing in Las Vegas* also makes numerous references to Horatio Alger and the American dream. Christopher Lehmann-Haupt called the work "a kind of mad, corrosive prose poetry that picks up where Norman Mailer's *An American Dream* [1965] left off."[24] Raoul Duke frequently looks to Alger for inspiration, asking himself at one point, "How would Horatio Alger handle this situation?"[25]

SELF-RELIANCE

Ralph Waldo Emerson's essay "Self-Reliance" (1841) provides a bridge between Franklin's *Autobiography* and Alger's rags-to-riches stories. Trained for the ministry, Emerson abandoned the pulpit for the podium, becoming one of the most popular lecturers of his day. Emerson's famous essays include "Nature" (1836), "The American Scholar" (1837), "The Divinity School Address" (1838), and "Experience" (1844), but "Self-Reliance" is his most renowned. In *The Invisible Man*, Mr. Norton recommends reading Emerson: "Self-reliance is a most worthy virtue," he tells the narrator. When a lover asks the eponymous heroine of *Susan Lenox* why she reads Emerson, she explains, "To find out about myself."[26] Susan Lenox was not alone in her reading tastes. Even before the nineteenth century came to a close, the image of the Emerson-reading woman was already a stereotype. In *Wheels and Whims* (1884), Connecticut novelist Florine Thayer McCray mentions "the traditional young woman of literary tastes, who is always decorated with a green veil, blue glasses, and a copy of Emerson."[27] And in *The Awakening* (1899), Kate Chopin has Edna Pontellier read Emerson, too.

"Self-Reliance" bristles with memorable passages, but Emerson did not coin the title phrase. The earliest known usage of the term "self-reliance" occurs in "Memoirs of Stephen Calvert," a serialized fiction by the leading Gothic novelist in American literature, Charles Brockden Brown.[28] But Emerson gave the phrase its currency. In "Self-Reliance," he offers a definition of genius: "To believe your own thought, to believe that what is true for you in your private heart, is true for all men,—that is genius." He stresses that people should assert their individuality and valorizes individual thought: "Nothing is at last sacred but the integrity of your own mind."[29] Emerson's concept of self-reliance strongly influenced such contemporary authors as Walt Whitman and Henry David Thoreau.

Emerson and Thoreau are the leading figures in the Transcendentalist movement, but their lives and works differ widely. Whereas Emerson's essay constitutes a theory of self-reliance, Thoreau's behavior provides the empirical proof verifying the theory.

Figure 1.5 S. A. Schoff, *Ralph Waldo Emerson*. An 1878 engraving after an original drawing by Sam W. Rowse, Library of Congress, Prints and Photographs Division (reproduction number LC-DIG-ppmsca-07398).

In short, Thoreau practiced what Emerson preached. Thoreau built his cabin at Walden Pond to see if he could live a self-sufficient life. He offered a carefully crafted version of that experience in *Walden; or, Life in the Woods* (1854).

Walden, the Transcendentalist's bible, belongs on everyone's list of books to read. But an image from Thoreau's earlier yet more difficult book, *A Week on the Concord and Merrimack Rivers* (1849), poignantly demonstrates the meaning of Transcendentalism. In the Tuesday chapter, Thoreau describes climbing Saddleback Mountain. After spending the night in the lookout tower at its peak, he awakens to see an ocean of mist reaching up to the base of the tower. The mist shuts out "every vestige of the earth" and leaves Thoreau "floating on this fragment of the wreck of a world, on my carved plank in cloudland." He continues:

> As the light in the east steadily increased, it revealed to me more clearly the new world into which I had risen in the night, the new terra-firma perchance of my future life. There was not a crevice left through which the trivial places we name Massachusetts, or Vermont, or New York, could be seen, while I still inhaled the clear atmosphere of a July morning,—if it were July there. All around beneath me was spread for a hundred miles on every side, as far as the eye could reach, an undulating country of clouds, answering in the varied swell of its surface to the terrestrial world it veiled.[30]

There, seated atop the clouds, Thoreau is able to transcend the earthly, to leave all the pettiness and crass materialism behind and commune with the gods. Transcendentalism is self-reliance elevated to the realm of metaphysics.

The act of transcending the earthly was fraught with psychic danger, as the "Ktaadn" chapter of Thoreau's *The Maine Woods*

(1865) suggests. Early in this chapter Thoreau welcomes readers to Maine. "Let those talk of poverty and hard times who will, in the towns and cities," he says. The man who goes to Maine could be "as rich as he pleases, where land virtually costs nothing, and houses only the labor of building, and he may begin life as Adam did."[31] Thoreau's words sound very like promotion literature: come to Maine, start life afresh, carve out a little piece of the wilderness for yourself, and become a new man. After climbing Mt. Ktaadn, he has a much different perspective.

No one could carve a niche from such wilderness, Thoreau explains upon coming down from the mountain. This part of America is "primeval, untamed, and forever untameable *Nature.*" Passing through an area ravaged by fire, he finds it no place for man. While intrigued with the burnt-out land, he feels uneasy. No longer communing with the gods as in *A Week*, he has become an interloper, a trespasser in the region of the gods. His psychic uncertainty prompts a crisis of identity as he exclaims: *"Contact! Contact! Who* are we? *where* are we?"[32] The ability to enter nature, become one with it, and thus transcend the quotidian, which had formed an integral part of *A Week* and *Walden*, disappears in the "Ktaadn" chapter of *The Maine Woods*. The American wilderness offers two possibilities to those in search of self. It could provide an exciting new sense of identity, or, alternatively, it could lead to the loss of self.

Regardless of the identity crisis Thoreau suffers in *The Maine Woods*, his writings, and Emerson's, have profoundly affected American culture. With the rise of the counterculture in the 1960s, the writings of Emerson and Thoreau underwent a huge revival, as a younger generation found in their words a philosophy for living a simpler life unfettered by the restraints of conventional society. One memorable phrase from "Self-Reliance" was adapted as a slogan of the counterculture. Emerson's words—"Do your thing, and I shall know you"—became "Do your own thing." Assert yourself. Create your own identity. From the time Captain John Smith first arrived in Virginia to the present, expressions of identity have formed an essential part of American literature.

Chapter 2

Travels

EIGHTEENTH-CENTURY TRAVELS

Once the initial work of colonization had been completed, American authors could traverse the colonies less as explorers and more as urbane travelers. Instead of being a matter of survival in a harsh environment among an unfamiliar race with unfamiliar customs, travel started to involve encounters with different types of early American colonists. With wit, vivacity, and sometimes condescension, travelers described whom they met and what they saw. This belletristic strain—travel literature written more to delight than instruct—starts with Sarah Kemble Knight and continues through William Byrd, Dr. Alexander Hamilton, and William Bartram. Eighteenth-century American authors established a rich tradition of travel writing that would continue through the coming centuries.

When Sarah Kemble Knight left Boston on an overland journey to New York in 1704, she kept a journal of her experience. Upon its initial publication in 1825, *The Journal of Madam Knight* was hailed as a major work of early American literature. Written when Increase Mather and his son Cotton controlled both the spiritual and cultural life of colonial Boston, Knight's journal is remarkably free from Puritan convention. Much early New England literature is devoted to interpreting the quotidian in terms of God's providence; Knight seems unfettered by such doctrinal tradition. Upon learning of an innkeeper named Mr. Devil, for instance, she has fun pondering whether she should "go to the Devil."[1]

Knight relates her experiences with charm and humor, playfulness and personality. Her powers of description are obvious from the outset. At one tavern she has difficulty finding a guide because the men there are "tyed by the Lipps to a pewter engine." Astride a skinny horse, the corpulent guide she finally finds resembles "a Globe on a Gate post." Forced to cross a swiftly flowing river in a canoe later in the narrative, she fears it will tip but safely endures. She makes light of the adventure, explaining that as she crossed she dared not "so much as to lodge my tongue a hair's breadth more on one side of my mouth than t'other."[2]

Since its initial publication, *The Journal of Madam Knight* has continued to amuse fun-loving readers and fellow writers. Donald Grant Mitchell, a popular nineteenth-century author best known by his pseudonym, Ik. Marvel, enjoyed Knight's "little thumbnail sketches of odd bumpkins," finding her ability to record "the very 'twang' of the country-side folk" droll, yet realistic.[3] More recently, T. Coraghessan Boyle used Knight's *Journal* as the basis for "The Doubtfulness of Water," a story forming part of a collection of his short fiction, *Tooth and Claw* (2005). Though Boyle has a reputation for his cynical humor, he stripped the funny bits from the *Journal* as he transformed Knight's personal story into a third-person narrative. He appears strangely unwilling to let Knight's literary ability upstage his own. In her *Journal*, Knight comes across as a woman who meets hardship with a smile on her face and a twinkle in her eye; in "The Doubtfulness of Water," she is a determined yet vulnerable woman seeking her way through a menacing wilderness.

William Byrd came from a much different background than Sarah Kemble Knight, but he, too, brought playfulness to travel writing, especially *The Secret History of the Line* and *The History of the Dividing Line*. These parallel works stem from the same journey. The Virginia–North Carolina border had been in dispute for years, but in 1728 commissioners were appointed to survey the line and settle the boundary. Byrd, a Virginia commissioner, led the survey. Like Knight's *Journal*, the *Secret History* was written for private circulation in manuscript. In this work, Byrd pokes fun at the seemingly crude and backward North Carolinians. This Virginia gentleman's derogatory jokes at the expense of neighboring colonists anticipate a teasing tradition of subsequent American humor between neighboring states. Much as Byrd laughs at North Carolinians, Ohioans would joke about West Virginians; people from Minnesota would make fun of those from Iowa. Such jokes show the inhabitants of each American colony or state defining themselves partly by defining their relationship with their neighbors. Paradoxically, intercolonial antagonism strengthened colonial unity.

Rewriting the *Secret History* into the *History*, which he intended to publish, Byrd minimized personal detail, but he inadvertently removed much of the story's charm. The surveying party went far enough west to encounter buffalo. In the *Secret History*, Steddy, Byrd's strong-willed, level-headed persona, explains: "Mrs. Mumford was so kind as to undertake to spin my Buffalo's Hair, in order to knit me a Pair of Stockins."[4] Byrd obviously enjoyed the idea of wearing sturdy buffalo socks. Afraid that such personal detail would make him seem jejune, he deflected attention from himself in revision. Speaking of buffalo wool in the *History*, Byrd observes, "Some People have Stockings knit of it, that would have serv'd an Israelite during his forty Years' march thro' the Wilderness."[5] The formality of the *History* excludes the picaresque delight of the *Secret History*.

Dr. Alexander Hamilton's *Itinerarium*, also written for private circulation, documents Hamilton's 1744 round-trip journey from Annapolis to Maine. Accompanied by his black slave Dromo—a Sancho Panza to his Don Quixote—Hamilton, wearing a lace hat, a green vest, ruffles, a brace of pistols, and a smallsword, cut quite a figure. An Edinburgh-trained physician, Hamilton is critical of the hicks he meets on the road, but the *Itinerarium* displays the complexity and variety of colonial American culture. Overall, it reads like a Whitmanesque celebration of American diversity as Hamilton portrays the different people he encounters: the Pennsylvanians who boast about the stoniness of their roads; the dancing, finical, humpbacked barber; the servant who has the audacity to get into a fistfight with his unwieldy, potbellied master; the comical fellow who is tolerably well versed in the quirps and quibbles of the law; the Dutch-speaking African woman who mouths off to Dromo; the young Boston man who mimics cats, dogs, cows, and hens, hitting notes high enough to bring his virility into question; the inquisitive rustic willing to purchase air to cure his fevers; and the drunken doctor who dares to spout against the renowned Dutch physician Herman Boerhaave.[6]

Possessing a charm all its own, William Bartram's *Travels* (1791) differs considerably from the humorous adventures of Knight, Byrd, and Hamilton. His father, John Bartram, the leading American naturalist of his generation, contributed to the field with *Observations on the Inhabitants, Climate, Soil, Rivers, Productions, Animals, and Other Matters* (1751), a hastily written and poorly edited work that is nonetheless chock-full of perceptive comments regarding both the American landscape and its native inhabitants.[7] Following in his father's footsteps, William Bartram made numerous botanical discoveries in the southeastern part of North America. Instead of organizing his work as a natural history, William Bartram chose to structure it as a travel narrative and thus embedded his discoveries in the text of his travels, making scientific discovery a part of action-packed adventure. His generous use of Latin scientific names to identify genus and species can be distracting at times, but sensitive readers accept this and even take pleasure in it. As James Dickey observes, "This cascade of identifications, the tumult of spirit-sounds descending from Rome, covers South Georgia and North Florida with Bartram's own kind of astonishment and love."[8]

William Bartram's curiosity is one of his most endearing qualities, but in the narrative it sometimes gets him into trouble. After making camp one afternoon, he sails to a nearby lagoon to catch fish, pausing to observe some alligators. At sunset, several alligators swim toward his boat. With a heavy club, he beats them away, but they redouble their force, surround him, and attempt to tip his canoe. After much peril, he safely reaches camp, where he must stay awake all night to guard against the sharp teeth of the encroaching alligators. Though the next day promises similar dangers and hardships, he delves deeper into alligator territory to continue his observations. Surviving this alligator gauntlet, he undergoes many more hairbreadth escapes as the narrative progresses.

Bartram's *Travels* thrilled contemporary British readers and powerfully influenced the British Romantics, especially William Wordsworth and Samuel Taylor Coleridge. Wordsworth's poetry sometimes recalls imagery from Bartram's *Travels*, and the diction of Coleridge's "Kubla Khan" is reminiscent of Bartram's description of the Isle of Palms.[9] Bartram gave English readers what many other contemporary travels lacked: exotic adventure.

CLASSICS OF THE WEST

American literature and the American landscape are indelibly linked. Though much of the continent remained unsettled through the colonial period, the expanse west of the Appalachians was still crucial to the development of the American mind. The wilderness fired the imagination: whenever settlers grew dissatisfied with their lives, they could imagine escaping further west and starting life anew. The West seemed like a place where dreams could come true. Responding to a British attack on American freedom, Benjamin Franklin said that if he could not defend his rights from where he lived, he would "retire chearfully with my little Family into the Boundless Woods of America which are sure to afford Freedom and Subsistance to any man who can bait a Hook or pull a Trigger."[10]

Few were more passionate about the West than Thomas Jefferson. In *Notes on the State of Virginia*, he foresaw the development of the Mississippi valley and the Missouri. As president, he organized the first transcontinental expedition. He pitched the Lewis and Clark expedition to Congress as a commercial venture but suggested that in the interest of international diplomacy, other nations should see the journey as one undertaken for "literary purposes," an adventure that would be written up and offered to the world as a contribution to science.

When Meriwether Lewis and William Clark triumphantly returned in 1806, Jefferson felt their work was only partway done. An excursion undertaken for literary purposes remained incomplete until an account of it was written and published. After their return, Nicholas Biddle began preparing the explorers' unwieldy journals for publication; Paul Allen finished the job. These two editors took the jumble of manuscripts and shaped them into a coherent narrative: *History of the Expedition Under the Command of Captains Lewis and Clark* (1814), a sprawling story with a panoramic sweep commensurate with the vastness of the continent.

Despite its breadth, *History of the Expedition* is vivid, even intimate, in its details. To their credit, Lewis and Clark recorded lively pen portraits of their experience, describing the land and its people in graphic detail. Editing their journals, Biddle and Allen recognized

Figure 2.1 Saint-Mémin, *Meriwether Lewis*. An engraving, circa 1805, Library of Congress, Prints and Photographs Division (reproduction number LC-USZ62-105848).

the freshness of the material and retained the raciness of the original. What becomes most apparent by the end of the story, however, is the dedication of the men who accompanied Lewis and Clark, their sense of accomplishment, and their understanding of the profound national significance of the journey. Many American poets have attempted to write epics that embody the majesty of their nation; *History of the Expedition* is such an American epic.

In *Commerce of the Prairies* (1844), Josiah Gregg presents a firsthand view of the Santa Fe Trail from the perspective of one who led several wagon trains along it. Gregg went to the West for his health but quickly fell in love with the land and the opportunities it offered. His account makes the West sound almost magical: it is a place where accepted rules of medicine do not apply, a place where people can restore their health solely by breathing the air. *Commerce of the Prairies* contrasts the unnecessarily complicated lifestyle of the civilized world with the elegant simplicity of prairie life. The early chapters critique such widely varying aspects of civilization as lace canopy beds and political parties. In the narrative, Gregg identifies several binary oppositions, all of which favor life in the West—luxury versus simplicity, indoors versus outdoors, unnatural versus natural, East versus West. According to Gregg, the "civilized" East has created false barriers that separate man from nature and man from man. Lacking such barriers, the West brings man and nature closer together and reasserts a natural harmony that the artificiality of civilization had impaired.

Another opposition established in the early pages of *Commerce of the Prairies* is characteristic of much nineteenth-century literary discourse: romance versus reality. Gregg's contrast between romance and reality functions similarly to others established early in the book. Much as a lace canopy creates a barrier between man and nature, much as political parties create barriers between men, romance is a false barrier that prevents people from facing truth. *Commerce of the Prairies* may start as a travel narrative, but it ultimately presents a philosophy of life.

By the time George Wilkins Kendall's *Narrative of the Texan Santa Fé Expedition* (1844) appeared, the story of the ill-fated military expedition was well known. A pioneering war correspondent, Kendall traveled with the Texas troops in the capacity of what in modern parlance would be called an embedded reporter. A sportsman and curiosity seeker, Kendall also wanted to learn about Indians and "participate in the wild excitement of buffalo-hunting, and other sports of the border and prairie life."[11] Little did he realize the grave consequences of his decision to come along.

Accompanying a foreign army—remember, this is the Republic of Texas—into hostile enemy territory, he assumed that he could pass unharmed because he was an American, an egotism that still afflicts American travelers.

In Kendall's *Narrative*, the troops get lost for weeks, often finding themselves near starvation. Once they reach New Mexico, they are taken prisoner and put under the charge of one Salazar, a despicable brute who starts them on a forced march to Mexico City: a journey of hardship, privation, despair, and death. Kendall's sense of humor helps him survive. His attempts at levity while a prisoner of war occasionally seem inappropriate, but dark humor belongs to an American tradition going back to Captain John Smith. Quoting the humorous yet disturbing cannibal episode from Smith's *General History of Virginia* (1624), Charles Dudley Warner sardonically identified Smith as "the first of the 'American humorists' who have handled subjects of this kind with such pleasing gayety."[12] From Smith to Kendall and beyond, dark humor has been a coping strategy, a defense mechanism useful for enduring otherwise unendurable horror.

Many stories of Western adventure follow a general pattern that takes the traveler on a path from innocence to experience. Osborne Russell vividly depicts his transformation from greenhorn to seasoned hunter in *Journal of a Trapper* (drafted 1847). When an incompetent leader gives him an order, Russell follows it to prove his courage, though it goes against both his personal judgment and the advice of seasoned mountain man Jim Bridger. Russell ends up alone in the wilderness, where he must fend for himself amid ferocious wolves. He places no further confidence in what his leader says. Instead, Russell uses his own knowledge and judgment to deliver himself from danger. After rejoining the other mountain men, who assume he has died,

Figure 2.2 Henry Bryan Hall, *Emigrants Crossing the Plain*. An 1869 engraving after an original painting by F.O.C. Darley, Library of Congress, Prints and Photographs Division (reproduction number LC-USZ62-730).

Russell discovers that his contract has expired, and he realizes he is now a free trapper. His transformation from serving as an employee to being his own boss constitutes a modern, capitalist version of the death-and-rebirth motif. With a sigh of relief, he announces that from this point forward he would be "independent of the world and no longer to be termed a 'Greenhorn.'"[13]

Francis Parkman deliberately situates *The Oregon Trail*—or, to use the first-edition title, *The California and Oregon Trail* (1849)—within the Romantic tradition. His title page epigraph comes from Byron, and chapter epigraphs derive from other Romantic poets, including a homegrown one, William Cullen Bryant. Parkman's chapter mottoes also align his work with Romantic fiction, especially the historical novels of James Fenimore Cooper, which helped to popularize their use. These bookish references provide a key for understanding *The Oregon Trail*.

Though recording his personal adventures, Parkman created a consciously literary work.

The Oregon Trail embodies the flavor and excitement of the American journey west, but throughout the narrative Parkman remains more observer than participant. In terms of outlook and attitude, he is closer to the dudes—the wealthy English travelers who came to the frontier for sport—than the emigrants. Parkman was unprepared for thunderstorms on the prairies, which were far more ferocious than any he had encountered in Boston. His poetic imagery and rhetorical skill bring the West alive for his readers. Between the time of his travels and the completion of his book, he reflected deeply on the experience and considered what it meant. *The Oregon Trail* achieves a level of respect often denied to travel literature. Reviewing the book, Herman Melville appreciated its ability to transport readers from their everyday lives: "He who desires to quit Broadway and the Bowery—though only in fancy— for the region of wampum and calumet, the land of beavers and buffaloes, birch canoes and 'smoked buckskin shirts' will do well to read Mr. Parkman's book."[14]

As the middle third of the nineteenth century gave way to the last, the Grand Canyon remained the only major area of unexplored American territory. In 1869, John Wesley Powell led an expedition successfully navigating the Colorado River. Two years later Powell organized a second expedition, one better able to endure the continual pounding inflicted by the fast-paced river and its nearly endless rapids and better equipped to undertake the surveying and mapmaking duties science demanded. *Exploration of the Colorado River* (1875) presents his results.

The latter part of the book contains the geological and topographical data, largely gathered during the second Powell expedition. The initial part, written as a day-to-day journal, tells the story of the first expedition, incorporating some detail from the second. Powell's composite narrative slights the efforts of the second expedition, but his attention to the first makes for a better story. After all, the fact that the river is unknown and unexplored is what gives the story its tension. The first explorers had no idea what they would encounter as they ventured downriver.

Frederick Dellenbaugh was only seventeen in 1871 when he began his river journey with Powell's second expedition. He, too, kept a journal. Three and a half decades would pass before he polished his journal into *A Canyon Voyage* (1908). Dellenbaugh's narrative contains much detail Powell omitted. As the journey begins in *A Canyon Voyage*, the men receive an ominous send-off when a deaf-mute pantomimes death, drowning, and disaster. Dellenbaugh's deaf-mute resembles both the prophetic Elijah in *Moby-Dick* and Lonnie, the crooked-eyed, banjo-playing albino boy in James Dickey's *Deliverance* (1970).

Dellenbaugh's narrative voice reflects his maturity while also portraying him as a teenage tenderfoot. He relates such episodes as naively mistaking grizzly bear tracks for human ones and making Dutch oven coffee cake with coffee grounds as the main ingredient. Often the simplest incidents reveal his growth into manhood. Relating how he learned to sew, Dellenbaugh explains that he cut some extraneous fabric from his swallow-tail coat and transferred the material to the knees and seat of his britches, where it could do more good.[15] With this episode, Dellenbaugh extends an American literary tradition: the celebration of patched clothing as a badge of honor goes back to "New England's Annoyances," an early seventeenth-century folk song.[16] Turning coattails into pants patches, Dellenbaugh abandons social convention for pragmatic purpose as he faces a new way of life, one in which fortitude takes precedence over fashion.

THE WORLD

American travelers have often used their experiences overseas not only to understand foreign lands but also to better understand their own culture. Frequently jingoistic, nineteenth-century travel narratives embody their authors' profound confidence in the American way of life. But the travel literature is too diverse and too vast to be reduced to generalization. Getting a handle on the huge number of travel texts published in the United States during the nineteenth century does present a formidable challenge.

In *American Travelers Abroad* (1999), an excellent bibliography of American travel writings before 1900, Harold Smith lists thousands of books from hundreds of authors. To sample a few of the more prominent ones from the middle of the century: Richard Henry Dana's *Two Years Before the Mast* (1840) presents the personal narrative of a Harvard-educated Boston Brahmin who dares to rub elbows with the mean mariners of the forecastle. *The Battle Summer: Being Transcripts from Personal Observations in Paris During the Year 1848* (1850), Donald Grant Mitchell's colorful eyewitness account of the French Revolution of 1848, registers its impact in both the political arena and the social sphere. William Wells Brown's *American Fugitive in Europe* (1855) tells the story of a runaway African American slave who exercises his freedom as he travels through France and Great Britain. John De Forest's *Oriental Acquaintance* (1856) consists of letters its author wrote from Syria, Palestine, and Lebanon during his time as a missionary. Nathaniel Hawthorne's *Our Old Home* (1863) collects sketches from its author's time in England. Henry James found *Our Old Home* "most delectable reading."[17] *The Marble Faun* (1860), the last novel Hawthorne published, might also be considered a work of travel literature: he pieced it together by excerpting big chunks of text from his Italian notebooks.

Works Harold Smith lists from the waning part of the century include David Ross Locke's *Nasby in Exile* (1882), a series of satirical letters that originally appeared in the *Toledo Blade* under Locke's renowned pen name, Petroleum V. Nasby; Lucy Bainbridge's *Round-the-World Letters* (1882), an epistolary account of an extraordinary journey that took her through Japan, China, India, the Holy Land, and Europe; seven works by Charles Dudley Warner, whom Smith finds alternately chatty and impressionistic but always displaying the light touch of an essayist;[18] and *The Innocents Abroad* (1869), *A Tramp Abroad* (1880), and *Following the Equator* (1897), three works by Mark Twain that, taken together, relate his world travels but also trace his intellectual journey from naïveté to cynicism.

The Holy Land attracted numerous American visitors through the nineteenth century, including John Lloyd Stephens, whose *Incidents of Travel in Egypt, Arabia Petraea, and the Holy Land* (1837) chronicles his sojourn in the land of Moses and Muhammad. Stephens views the antiquities of the Near East from a modern perspective. A man of his times, he has little patience for ceremony, takes pride in American know-how, and exudes confidence in the enormous potential of modern technology. Though Stephens favorably compares the United States with the Near East, he reaches a point while crossing the desert on a camel when he questions the value of technology. Foreseeing the day when locomotives will replace camels, he observes, "When that day comes, all the excitement and wonder of a journey in the desert will be over."[19]

In one memorable episode, Stephens endures extreme hunger and thirst while crossing the desert. With tremendous relief he spies a single palm tree in the distance, which proves to be his salvation. Stephens's contemporary readers vividly remembered the episode. In *Redburn* (1849), Herman Melville's fictional retelling of a youthful voyage to Liverpool, Stephens makes a cameo appearance. One day Wellingborough Redburn's aunt points him out in church, teasing the boy with a tall tale. "See what big eyes he has," she whispers, "they got so big, because when he was almost dead with famishing in the desert, he all at once caught sight of a date tree, with the ripe fruit hanging on it."[20]

By the time he wrote *Redburn*, his fourth book, Melville understood how to reshape the story of his peregrinations into a novel. *Typee* (1846), his first book, appeared as part of the Library of American Books, a prestigious series edited by Evert Duyckinck and published by Wiley and Putnam.[21] With *Typee*, Melville tested the boundaries of the travel narrative, seeing how far he could stretch the truth and get away with it. In the process, he created a charming, and enduring, work. Frederick Dellenbaugh describes the process of reading *Typee* as being "lost in its wonderful glow."[22] Many contemporary readers questioned the book's veracity, however. Melville's fanciful description partly explains why, but some British readers questioned its truthfulness for another reason. Reflecting deeply ingrained class prejudices, they considered *Typee* too well written to be the work of someone who sailed before the mast.

Typee retells the story of Melville and his friend Richard Tobias Greene, who had jumped ship together when their whaling vessel touched at Nukuheva in the Marquesas. After escaping into the lush undergrowth, they traveled overland, ending up among the supposedly cannibalistic Typee natives. Lameness incapacitated Melville; Greene left for help but never returned. Melville stayed a few more weeks, not months as in *Typee*, but eventually signed aboard a passing Australian whaler that brought him to Tahiti, an experience inspiring his second book, *Omoo* (1847).

Those contemporary readers who took issue with Melville's deliberate fictionalizations included Commodore Matthew

Calbraith Perry. Finding himself in Liverpool after his unprecedented diplomatic mission, which opened Japan to the Occident, Perry visited the American consulate, where he asked Nathaniel Hawthorne to recommend someone to write up his journey to Japan. Hawthorne, who had performed a similar task when he edited Horatio Bridge's *Journal of an African Cruiser* (1845), suggested his friend Herman Melville, but Perry felt that Melville lacked the gravitas necessary for the task. He chose Francis Lister Hawks instead.

An Episcopal clergyman whose works include *The Monuments of Egypt* (1850), a narrative of a voyage up the Nile, Hawks could give the story of Perry's diplomatic mission to Japan the gravity it deserved. To create *Narrative of the Expedition of an American Squadron to the China Seas and Japan* (1856) Hawks performed a task similar to what Nicholas Biddle and Paul Allen did for Lewis and Clark. He took Perry's journal, those of his officers, and the official reports and combined them into a unified work, which gave American readers the fullest picture of Japan they had ever read. To his credit, Hawks included much scientific and diplomatic detail, but he managed to infuse the narrative with the romance of travel. His depiction of the folkways of the Japanese people shaped American attitudes toward the Orient for years to come.

Since the Civil War had kept Americans home, the war's end prompted a huge boom in European travel. Several travelers wrote up their stories for publication, but one towers above the rest: Henry James. Best known as an author of highly nuanced, psychologically intricate novels, James developed a parallel career as a travel writer. For him the two genres played off each other. His time in Europe provided inspiration for novels and substance for books of travel. James's novels are sensitive portraits of the types of people he met in Europe; alternatively, his travel books are, to borrow the title of one, portraits of places.

Figure 2.3 *Commodore Perry in Japan*. Woodcut print on hosho paper, undated. Library of Congress, Prints and Photographs Division (reproduction number LC-USZ62-519).

The publication of James's novels and corresponding travel books closely coincided. *Transatlantic Sketches*, which details his 1872 trip to Europe, appeared in early 1875, the same year he serialized *Roderick Hudson*, the story of a New England sculptor and his patron who travel to Rome with tragic results. In 1881, James published *The Portrait of a Lady*, a sprawling novel relating the story of several characteristic American types who gather in Europe around Isabel Archer, the young lady of the title. Some of the characters are autobiographical projections, while others recall people James met during his travels in Europe; yet others, especially the villainous Gilbert Osmond, are the brilliant inventions of the author. In 1882, James traveled through Touraine, Languedoc, and Provence, which he chronicled in *A Little Tour in France* (1884). *Portraits of Places* (1883) collects several travel articles James previously published in magazines. Though his books of travel have not achieved the lasting fame of his fiction, many contemporary readers preferred his travel writing over his novels.

A Little Tour in France starts in Tours, the birthplace of French novelist Honoré de Balzac. No other author was more important to James, as the many respectful references in *A Little Tour* clarify. But it is the places, not the people, that James prefers to discuss in his travel books. He was intrigued with the way France's cathedrals, châteaus, and various other assorted architectural curiosities reflected the nation's character. His natural descriptions are no less beautiful or striking than his architectural ones. Sometimes the people that appear in *Little Tour* seem like pawns for James to move where he wills. In Loches, for example, he sees a huge horse chestnut tree, "a tree of a circumference so vast and so perfect that the whole population of Loches might sit in concentric rows beneath its boughs."[23] *A Little Tour* ends in a city park in Dijon, and James's low-key conclusion suits the understated tone of the whole book. He depicts himself quietly sitting on a Dijon park bench shortly before boarding the express back to Paris. As the sun sets and darkness blurs the scenery, his memories of travel become more distinct. James beautifully captures the not unpleasing sadness that contemplative travelers feel toward the end of any trip.

A contemporary bicyclist suggested *A Little Tour* would make "a capital hand-book for cyclists in France."[24] The suggestion indicates that by the mid-1880s, bicycling had become a viable mode of transportation for adventuresome travelers. Thomas Stevens chronicled his round-the-world bicycle tour for *Outing* magazine. Starting from San Francisco, he pedaled across the continent to New York. After sailing the Atlantic, he resumed his tour, cycling through Europe, Turkey, Persia, Afghanistan, India, China, and Japan. The serialized version of his story made Stevens famous. By the time his narrative appeared in book form as *Around the World on a Bicycle* (1887–88), his reputation as both a traveler and a writer was firmly established throughout the United States. Stevens lacks James's subtlety and sense of style, but his narrative brings alive the thrill of bicycle touring. For instance, Stevens enjoyed the fresh air after a rainstorm as he cycled through the rolling French countryside; he compares the charming experience with tobogganing in Canada.[25]

Stevens sought an alternative mode of travel for a subsequent adventure. *Through Russia on a Mustang* (1891) documents his eleven-hundred-mile ride on a temperamental Hungarian steed. His Russian sojourn pales before that of George Kennan, who took several arduous journeys across Russia. After the first attempt to lay an Atlantic telegraph cable failed, Western Union decided to establish telegraph service between America and Europe the long way: overland across Siberia. Kennan joined the ambitious expedition and chronicled his experience in *Tent Life in Siberia* (1870), a popular book that established his reputation as a travel writer.

Tent Life records the dogged determination of Kennan and his men to lay the cable. Although they had devoted three years to the project, another attempt to lay a telegraph cable across the Atlantic succeeded, so all Kennan's hard work went for naught.

TWENTIETH-CENTURY TRAVELS

Through the nineteenth century, guidebooks had been useful aids for American travel writers, but in the twentieth, some guidebooks took on literary qualities themselves. The Federal Writers' Project, which formed part of Franklin D. Roosevelt's Works Progress Administration, hired writers to fan out across the nation, interviewing people and researching places. The result was the American Guide series, which consists of beefy guidebooks for every state and a variety of specialized volumes. Many prominent or soon-to-be prominent authors worked for the Federal Writers'

Figure 2.4 George Kennan, *A Siberian Posting Sledge Drawn by Three Horses*. Photographic print, 1885–1886. Library of Congress, George Kennan Papers (reproduction number LC-USZ62-128129).

Project, including Conrad Aiken, Nelson Algren, Saul Bellow, Arna Bontemps, John Cheever, Jack Conroy, Ralph Ellison, Zora Neale Hurston, Eudora Welty, and Richard Wright.[26]

Figure 2.5 *Illinois: A Descriptive and Historical Guide.* Silkscreen print, 1940. Library of Congress, Work Projects Administration Poster Collection (reproduction number LC-USZC2-5191).

Since the guides were published anonymously, the efforts of these individual contributors have been obscured, but the separate volumes possess a general literary quality otherwise rare for guidebooks. Beautiful imagery and figurative language abound. Take *The Ohio Guide* (1940), for instance. The section devoted to Toledo emphasizes the importance of the Maumee River to the city and, in so doing, creates a beautiful little vignette: "The broad curving river that gradually widens into the bay is, and always has been, the heart and highway of the city. From the breakup of the ice in spring until winter halts navigation, boats ranging in size from 700-foot ore freighters to saucy catboats go busily up and down the waterway."[27]

John Steinbeck testified to the value of the American Guide series. Steinbeck's own contributions to American travel writing include *Sea of Cortez* (1941), a narrative of a journey to Cabo San Lucas co-written with Ed Ricketts, who would inspire the character of Doc in *Cannery Row* (1945); *A Russian Journal* (1948), an illustrated account of a journey Steinbeck took with photographer Robert Capa; and *Travels with Charley: In Search of America* (1962), which describes his journey across the United States in a camper named Rocinante (after Don Quixote's superannuated steed) with a French poodle named Charley. In *Travels with Charley*, Steinbeck proclaims, "If there had been room in Rocinante I would have packed the W.P.A. Guides to the States . . . The complete set comprises the most comprehensive account of the United States ever got together, and nothing since has even approached it."[28]

To represent the second half of the century, one final travel writer must suffice. Few other twentieth-century Americans have traveled as widely or written as well as Paul Theroux. *The Great Railway Bazaar* (1975), his first book of travel, relates the story of his railway excursion across Europe, the Middle East, India, Southeast Asia, Japan, Mongolia, and the Soviet Union. In *The*

Old Patagonian Express (1979), Theroux describes his journey from Massachusetts to the southern tip of South America. In *The Kingdom by the Sea* (1983), he presents a trip around the perimeter of Britain. Subsequent journeys have taken him to China, India, the South Pacific, and the Mediterranean.

Borrowing his title for *The Kingdom by the Sea* from Poe's "Annabel Lee" and using an epigraph from Henry James, Theroux clearly situates himself within the American literary tradition. Like Poe and James, he, too, is a novelist. All three authors pride themselves on their craftsmanship. Curiously for a travel writer, Theroux puts more emphasis on people than places. *The Kingdom by the Sea* contains numerous character sketches and even prints snippets of conversation. But sometimes Theroux seems content to observe other people and, instead of getting to know them, to invent names and personalities for them. Though Theroux has traveled to the ends of the earth, he never fully escapes the self-regard that has afflicted Americans abroad since the days of John Lloyd Stephens.

Teachers of American literature have long understood the value travel writing holds for the history of colonial American writing, but the novels and short stories and poetry of the nineteenth and twentieth centuries often muscle books of travel off the syllabus. They shouldn't. Any piece of writing that approaches excellence can be considered literature regardless of genre. Indeed, there may be more literature in William Bartram's description of an alligator attack, Francis Parkman's account of a thunderstorm traversing the plains, or John Stephens's narrative of hunger in the desert than can be found in any number of nineteenth-century novels. American travel writing can fire the imagination and take readers around the globe.

Chapter 3

Autobiography

THE EXAMPLE OF BENJAMIN FRANKLIN

Benjamin Franklin began writing his autobiography, the most famous autobiography in American literature, in London in 1771. He continued its composition off and on until his death nineteen years later. Typically read as one of his last writings, it really belongs within the context of his literary, social, and political activities of the late 1760s and early 1770s. The work's primary motivation is much the same as the one underlying Franklin's political writings of the early 1770s: his autobiography constitutes an impassioned defense of the American way of life. In the face of British encroachments, Franklin upheld his own life to show what a person could accomplish in America. He comes across as a new kind of man, one whose characteristic behavior transcends the class boundaries that traditionally had separated one person from another.

Discussing a childhood episode early in the autobiography, Franklin explains his fascination with the way craftsmen handle their tools, something that continued to intrigue him throughout his life. His celebration of American craftsmen looks forward to Walt Whitman's celebration of American workers in "Song of Myself." By carefully observing them, Franklin learned how to do little jobs on his own when he could not find a workman. He personally embodied the handyman spirit that thrives today in the do-it-yourself ethos. His practical knowledge also let him build basic machines to conduct his electrical experiments. Directly linking his affinity with the workingman and his scientific pursuits in the narrative, Franklin reveals their continuity. In his day, the pursuit of science was an amateur activity, an endeavor undertaken by the gentleman-virtuoso. Demonstrating that his knowledge of craftsmen's tools facilitated his gentlemanly pursuit of science, Franklin demolishes class distinctions between the craftsman and the gentleman.[1]

Education usually served to separate the classes, but Franklin's autobiography reveals how his process of self-education helped him transcend class barriers. His discussion of reading, complete with the names of authors and titles of books he read, presents readers with a program of study they can follow themselves.

Figure 3.1 *The Reception of Benjamin Franklin in France.* Chromolithograph, 1882. Library of Congress, Prints and Photographs Division (reproduction number LC-DIG-pga-00475).

Describing his friends, Franklin reinforces the importance of books. Nearly all of them loved to read—a personal characteristic sufficient to endear them to him. Franklin made friends easily; the affectionate tone he takes in the autobiography makes him seem like the reader's friend. The book first appeared in a French translation in the early 1790s and in English soon afterward. It became an instant classic and has since been translated into dozens of languages. It has never gone out of print.

Tom Wolfe calls autobiography "the one form of nonfiction that has always had most of the powers of the novel."[2] He is not necessarily saying that autobiographers deliberately fictionalize their life stories, though some do. Charles Mingus, for one, prefaces his autobiography, *Beneath the Underdog* (1971), with the following note: "Some names in this work have been changed and some of the characters and incidents are fictitious." For most autobiographers, the writing process is a matter of selection, not imagination. Starting with the various events that have shaped their lives, they choose the ones that let them tell the version of their life story they wish to tell. Franklin omitted some famous episodes in his life to stress those displaying him as a humble and hardworking printer. He presents himself in the *Autobiography* as an example to be imitated. The scheme worked: his is the prototypical story of the self-made man, and it set a pattern many American autobiographies would follow.

SPIRITUAL AUTOBIOGRAPHY AND CAPTIVITY NARRATIVES

The autobiographical tradition was deeply ingrained in American culture well before Franklin put pen to paper. It was crucial to the belief system and devotional practice of the New England Puritans.

Following the basic tenets of Calvinism, they believed that only a part of the population formed God's elect. To mitigate a faith that could turn toward bleak determinism, the Puritans also believed that God would reveal their blessedness to them. Loath to communicate with man directly, God, according to Puritan belief, used an elaborate system of natural signs to express himself. Recognizing and understanding these signs took considerable vigilance and interpretive skill on the Puritans' part. They stayed on the lookout for anything extraordinary that could be interpreted as a sign from God. Many kept spiritual diaries to record these instances of divine providence. Such diaries formed the basis for their spiritual autobiographies, which they would present to their congregations before obtaining full membership in the church.

Typical of the Puritans' spiritual outlook, Thomas Shepard's *Autobiography* rises above others in terms of both its bold imagery and its brave rhetoric. College students today may relate to the formative experiences Shepard records in his spiritual autobiography, which he completed around 1646. As an undergraduate at Emmanuel College, Cambridge, he encountered some loose company. One Saturday night he got so drunk that, as he explains, "I . . . knew not where I was until I awakened late on that Sabbath and sick with my beastly carriage."[3] This disconcerting experience turned him to daily meditation and thus set him on a path toward a more righteous life.

After college Shepard started preaching, but his beliefs diverged widely from those of the established church. He found himself increasingly persecuted in England. To save himself and his family, he decided to emigrate to New England. The death-and-rebirth theme that would become such a prevalent motif in American literature is central to Shepard's personal story. Relating his first attempt to reach New England, he explains how he was miraculously saved from near-certain shipwreck, concluding the episode: "This deliverance was so great that I then did think if ever the Lord did bring me to shore again I should live like one come and risen from the dead."[4] As the story progresses, he finally reaches New England, where he can do God's work.

Closely allied to spiritual autobiography, the captivity narrative constituted a form of popular literature in colonial America. Captivity narratives do not have to be spiritual: Captain John Smith's famous story of his capture by Powhatan and rescue by Pocahontas is not. But nearly all colonial New England captivity narratives are. Captives usually depicted their personal stories of survival as instances of divine providence. In Mary Rowlandson's case, devotion to God shows throughout *A Narrative of the Captivity and Restauration of Mrs. Mary Rowlandson* (1682), but other aspects of the work contribute to its literary quality.

Rowlandson is an excellent storyteller. The Indian attack that begins *A Narrative* is as thrilling, as poignant, as gory as anything in James Fenimore Cooper or Sam Peckinpah. Graphic violence is not necessarily what makes her narrative a lasting work of literature. Her personality and her ability to convey that personality elevate *A Narrative* over other stories of captivity. Rowlandson emerges as a strong, forceful woman who asserts her personality and maintains her dignity even when threatened with starvation or physical harm. She knows what she must do to survive and does it. In *A Narrative*, she thanks God profusely for delivering her from danger, but by its end, Rowlandson herself seems more responsible than anyone else for getting her through the trying experience.

SLAVE NARRATIVES

Like the captivity narrative, the slave narrative is another genre of American autobiography revealing the racial and social tensions endemic to American culture. One towers above all others:

Narrative of the Life of Frederick Douglass, An American Slave (1845). Douglass begins the story with his birth: "I was born in Tuckahoe, near Hillsborough, and about twelve miles from Easton, in Talbot county, Maryland. I have no accurate knowledge of my age, never having seen any authentic record containing it."[5] By itself, Douglass's opening sentence is unremarkable, but as his narrative continues to the next sentence, it gathers momentum. The second sentence, which explains that Douglass cannot place himself in time, reveals the purpose of the first sentence's geographical precision: to situate himself in space. The absence of authentic documentary evidence prevented Douglass from knowing when he was born; writing the autobiography, he created a document authenticating the self.

Figure 3.2 *Frederick Douglass.* Photographic print, undated. Library of Congress, Prints and Photographs Division (reproduction number LC-USZ62-15887).

Enhancing the literary sophistication of *Narrative of the Life*, Douglass uses different modes of discourse to tell his story. He draws upon the oral tradition and incorporates numerous proverbs.[6] He experiments with such literary styles as sentimentalism and gothic horror, sometimes using the two in conjunction. Describing his master's wife, who had never owned slaves before her marriage, Douglass invokes the imagery of sentimental fiction: "Her face was made of heavenly smiles, and her voice of tranquil music."[7] Dark gothic imagery takes over once marriage gives her slaves of her own. Douglass relates what happened to her after she turns into a slave owner. She "became red with rage; that voice, made all of sweet accord, changed to one of harsh and horrid discord; and that angelic face gave place to that of a demon."[8] In other words, slavery changes a sentimental ideal into a horrific monster. *Narrative of the Life* provides many similar examples. Douglass brilliantly manipulates the conventions of popular literature to tell a story that moved contemporary abolitionists and readers with its author's ability to turn a phrase and turn the tide of public sentiment.

Other slave narratives have been recognized as landmarks in American literary history. Few have received more attention than *Interesting Narrative of the Life of Olaudah Equiano* (1789). Long accepted as an authentic account of Olaudah Equiano's life, *Interesting Narrative* and its author have undergone intense critical scrutiny lately. Scholars now question the veracity of many details. Equiano claimed he was born in Africa; new documentary evidence suggests that he was born in the Carolinas instead.[9] The recent controversy over the narrative has only served to enhance its literary complexity. *Interesting Narrative* is now seen as a composite work, a collective autobiography that draws on the experiences of any and all African Americans Equiano knew. Using the lives of others to write his own autobiography, Equiano claims the right to speak for all slaves.

SECULAR NARRATIVES

Louis Kaplan's *Bibliography of American Autobiographies* (1961), the standard reference in the field, lists more than six thousand book-length works through 1945. Mary Louise Briscoe's follow-up, *American Autobiography, 1945–1980: A Bibliography* (1982), lists thousands more. A quick glance through Kaplan's occupational index reveals how wide-ranging the field is. He lists autobiographies of abolitionists and actors, alcoholics and athletes, bankers, bicyclists, bums (but no bicycle bums), cabinet makers, cabinet members, cantors, cattlemen and clergymen, college presidents and college students, cowboys, detectives, cowboy-detectives, engineers, farmers, gamblers, hunters, journalists, lawyers, lumberjacks, novelists, painters, photographers, preachers and sailors, teachers and whalers, and many, many, many more. The length of these various autobiographies is uneven, their quality even more so, but all reflect a similar impulse: to tell others the story of the self.

Many of the works Briscoe and Kaplan list have been recognized as major contributions to the genre. *The Education of Henry Adams* (1907) may be best remembered for Adams's insightful contrast between the Virgin Mary and the electric dynamo, both symbols of power, one representing the religious faith of the past, the other symbolizing the force of modern science and technology. In *Twenty Years at Hull House* (1910), Jane Addams, the groundbreaking social reformer, relates her strenuous efforts to found the Hull House settlement in Chicago. Hamlin Garland's *Son of the Middle Border* (1917), a classic of the Midwest, is the greatest work of a prolific novelist who found his true métier when he shifted from fiction to memoir.

Several acclaimed autobiographies appeared in the 1940s, including Zora Neale Hurston's *Dust Tracks on a Road* (1942).

A carefully crafted narrative written in a deceptively unpolished style, Hurston's autobiography portrays her personal struggle using a combination of folk humor and richly detailed imagery. Frank Lloyd Wright's *An Autobiography* (1932; rev. ed., 1943) tells the story of the nation's most renowned architect. While the structure of his narrative lacks the elegance of his buildings, Wright's articulation of his professional ideals is impressive. He emerges from his autobiography as a man profoundly dedicated to his craft. His passion and creativity encourage readers to cultivate their own artistic interests.

Woody Guthrie's *Bound for Glory* (1943) re-creates in rough-hewn vernacular the rough-and-tumble world of this Oklahoma-born folk singer. Hopping freight trains, hitching rides, tramping penniless for miles and days, Guthrie echoes the vagabond poetry of Bliss Carman and Vachel Lindsay and anticipates the spontaneous prose of Jack Kerouac. When a friend loaned Bob Dylan a copy of *Bound for Glory*, he devoured it. Recalling the book in *Chronicles* (2004), the first volume of his own autobiography, Dylan could hardly come up with enough similes to convey his enthusiasm for the book: "I went through it from cover to cover like a hurricane, totally focused on every word, and the book sang out to me like the radio."[10]

Some of the more obscure autobiographies that Kaplan lists deserve more renown, works such as *The Life of Black Hawk* (1833), the frustrating personal story of the Sauk warrior who resisted American encroachments onto Indian lands for decades; Annie Nelles's *Life of a Book Agent* (1868), which relates her daring experiences selling books door-to-door during the mid-nineteenth century, a time when many women scarcely ventured beyond their own front door; John Wesley Clampitt's *Echoes from the Rocky Mountains* (1889), a savory tale of an attorney employed by the Justice Department to track down mail robbers in the West; Charles Eliot Goodspeed's *Yankee Bookseller* (1937), which

Figure 3.3 *Black Hawk*. Chromolithograph, 187?. Library of Congress, Prints and Photographs Division (reproduction number LC-USZC4-3255).

presents a series of piquant anecdotes of book buying and selling in early twentieth-century Boston; and Salom Rizk's *Syrian Yankee* (1943), one of many immigrant autobiographies that convey a passion for American freedom sometimes lost on those native-born citizens who take their freedom for granted. Born in Syria, Rizk emigrated to the United States as a teen, settling with an uncle in Iowa. Three years after his arrival, he had mastered English and started a career as an inspirational speaker. *Syrian Yankee* presents an expanded version of its author's speeches: the written text retains Rizk's easygoing conversational style and his capacity to inspire.

AUTOBIOGRAPHY AND THE PROBLEM OF AUTHORSHIP

Autobiography presents a unique problem in terms of authorship. By definition, an autobiography is a biography written by its subject. Since people with great stories to tell are not necessarily great writers, they seek the help of others to ghostwrite, or at least to help write, their autobiographies. Do these ghostwritten autobiographies deserve consideration as literature? Should they be considered autobiography? To omit them from consideration would be to exclude some of the finest biographical writing in American literature. Their authorship may be problematic, but the cooperative nature of their composition has often led to some very special books. The best ghostwriters feed off the adventures, accomplishments, and anecdotes of their subjects, turning raw biographical material into compelling narrative.

Samuel S. McClure's *My Autobiography* (1914) was ghosted by a woman who now ranks among the finest American novelists of the twentieth century: Willa Cather. McClure, a prominent publisher and magazinist, approached Cather with the project in 1913, the year she published *O Pioneers!*, the novel that established the tone of nostalgia for the early days of Nebraska settlement that would echo throughout her oeuvre. Speaking with her, McClure related his personal story, something he had told and retold countless times on the lecture circuit. *My Autobiography* is thus a product of a well-rehearsed oral narrative and careful shaping by a consummate literary stylist.

In the book, Cather expresses McClure's passage from youth to adulthood in a way many Americans could appreciate. Taking his first job out of college, as the story goes, McClure leaves his young, idealistic self behind. Somehow that young self still exists, but McClure can no longer identify with him. He came east; the younger self retreated west. Overall, *My Autobiography* is very much a celebration of the American Midwest, its people and the wholesome values they represent. Cather's portrayal differs considerably from the way the region had been depicted in earlier literature. *My Autobiography* and *O Pioneers!* thus reflect a similar attitude toward the West. No longer the land of opportunity, it is a land of youthful idealism, a land of memory. What the West formerly represented has receded into the past.

McClure autographed Cather's presentation copy of *My Autobiography* as follows: "With affectionate regard for the real author." Nowhere in the book's printed text does he acknowledge her authorship.[11] In recent decades, autobiographers have been more willing to thank their collaborators, sometimes on the title page or at least in the acknowledgments. The title page of Jake La Motta's *Raging Bull* (1970), for instance, shows that La Motta co-wrote it with Joseph Carter and Peter Savage. Carter, a professional writer, polished the prose and put on the finishing touches, but Savage's contributions may be more influential. A longtime friend who figures prominently in the book as Pete, Savage was a partner in Jake's early criminal activities and also in his subsequent success as a boxer. Discussing Savage's influence on the book, Martin Scorsese observed, "He put a dramatic structure on Jake's chaotic existence. It wasn't so much Jake speaking about himself as Pete explaining Jake to Jake!"[12]

The structure of the book makes the story quite disturbing. Here's its opening sentence: "There was this bookie, Harry Gordon."[13] This one will never make it onto a list of classic first sentences in American literature, but it introduces a man who figures prominently in the initial chapter, which depicts La Motta beating up Gordon, who typically carried around a large wad of cash. In the second chapter, Jake reads a news item relating that Harry died from the beating and also that his assailant had overlooked $1,700 Harry had on him.

After quoting the news item, which he had read in a bodega, Jake asks a rhetorical question: "Have you ever been belted, hard, right in the throat? It paralyzes you. You can't do anything, even breathe. That was me, standing there in that little store."[14] Jake's reaction is ambiguous. Is he shocked because he murdered Harry or because he missed the wad? Either way, Jake puts his readers in a quandary. Is he really confessing to a murder in this book? No, as things turned out. About three-quarters of the way through the narrative, Harry Gordon, alive and well, shows up, explaining to Jake that the newspaper that had reported his death was mistaken. Readers may be relieved to know they have not, after all, been reading the autobiography of a murderer, but they may remain disturbed that they have followed the story for so long before learning this fact, and that they could read it intensely enough to identify with a murderer.

JAZZ AUTOBIOGRAPHY

Modern celebrity culture has triggered an exponential growth in American autobiography. While celebrity autobiographies merit study as a cultural phenomenon, few possess literary stature. There is one subset that may share literature's staying power: jazz autobiography. These self-told personal stories of jazz musicians are starting to receive attention from both musicologists and literary historians, who not only recognize their documentary value but also see in them transcendental aesthetic qualities.[15] Louis Armstrong initiated this subgenre with *Swing That Music* (1936), but since then dozens of jazz musicians have related their adventures and experience.

Figure 3.4 *Louis Armstrong*. Photographic print, 1953. New York World-Tele-gram and the Sun Newspaper Photograph Collection, Library of Congress (reproduction number LC-USZ62-127236).

Swing That Music intertwines Armstrong's personal story with the history of jazz, but sometimes it seems less like autobiography or history and more like myth. In terms of both theme and motif, it shares qualities with much of American literature. The title of the opening chapter, "Jazz and I Get Born Together," emphasizes that jazz developed and Armstrong matured simultaneously. Armstrong states that he was born in New Orleans on July 4, 1900, a fact that reinforces jazz's essential American roots. Instead of starting his story on the Fourth of July, however, Armstrong begins it on a day with more personal resonance: New Year's Eve thirteen years later, a night when he shot off a.38 Special, got arrested, and was sent to the Waif's Home for Boys, where he joined the brass band and learned to play the trumpet.

After leaving the boys' home, he pursued his music, taking many different gigs around New Orleans. Performing with a jazz band in the back of a truck as an advertising stunt one evening, he encountered another band on another truck. Suddenly an impromptu jazz competition began. After this chance meeting, the Fates intervened, or to be precise, one Fate—that is, Fate Marable, a jazz pianist and bandleader, who was so impressed with Armstrong's trumpet playing on the truck he hired him to play on the *Dixie Belle*, an excursion boat heading north on the Mississippi. The spirit of Mark Twain hovers over the journey. Having read *Tom Sawyer* at the boys' home, Armstrong remembers Jackson's Island, where Tom Sawyer and his gang pretended to be pirates. To Armstrong's surprise, the grizzled captain of the *Dixie Belle* claims to have known Twain personally. As in *Huckleberry Finn*, the river journey in *Swing That Music* symbolizes the growth of the hero. When they reach Jackson's Island, the captain points it out to Armstrong, but the world of Tom Sawyer now seems like the distant past. The romance of youth has disappeared, and Jackson's Island looks just like any other island in the Mississippi.

Jazz autobiographies present the same problems of authorship as many other modern autobiographies. Often their authors have had help from co-authors or ghostwriters. W. C. Handy, the pioneering blues musician and composer, dictated *Father of the Blues* (1941), and Arna Bontemps edited the manuscript. According to the title page, Billie Holiday wrote *Lady Sings the Blues* (1956) with William Dufty. And *Good Morning Blues* (1985), Count Basie's autobiography, is an as-told-to narrative written by Albert Murray. Some are constructed from tape recordings. Alan Lomax, best known as a folk music collector, assembled *Mister Jelly Roll* (1950) from numerous tape-recorded tales by early jazz pianist and composer Jelly Roll Morton. Explaining his editorial process, Lomax said that he transferred "the surge of speech into the quieter flow of type," a process that could create prose "as graceful and finely-tuned as the best of written literature."[16]

Treat It Gentle (1960), the autobiography of the prominent New Orleans clarinetist Sidney Bechet, is based on tape recordings transcribed and edited by John Ciardi, Desmond Flower, and Joan Reid. Ciardi, a distinguished poet and translator, applied his literary skills to transfer Bechet's spoken word into a written text that sometimes reads like poetry. *Treat It Gentle* resembles a sequel to *The Grandissimes* (1880), George Washington Cable's masterful novel that anatomizes Creole society in New Orleans at the time of the American acquisition of Louisiana. Devoting much space to his grandfather's story, Bechet uses some of the same New Orleans legends Cable had used in his novel—but Bechet tells them from an African American perspective. *Treat It Gentle* is questionable as documentary evidence of Bechet's life; as literature, it represents jazz autobiography at its finest.

Miles Davis wrote *Miles* (1989) with Quincy Troupe, according to the title page. Though the overuse of profanity, the frequent redundancies, the occasional clichés, and the conversational tone all lend the narrative an aura of authenticity, do not be fooled by *Miles*. Troupe explains the nature of the narrative in his afterword. He spent many hours interviewing his subject, but unlike *Mister Jelly Roll*, *Miles* is *not* a transcription of interview tapes. Rather, it is Troupe's attempt to write the way Davis talked, which was the same way Troupe's father and many other African American men of his father's generation talked. Troupe explains: "I grew up listening to them on street corners, in barbershops, ball parks and gymnasiums, and bucket-of-blood bars. It's a speaking style that I'm proud and grateful to have documented."[17] The obscene language generated controversy when the book first appeared, mainly because it differed so much from mainstream jazz discourse, which typically maintains a respectful, even highfalutin tone. Troupe dared to publish *Miles* in the language Davis and other jazz musicians spoke outside public earshot.[18]

As the body of jazz autobiography grows, it naturally grows more intricate. Recent autobiographies make allusions to earlier ones and create a kind of dialogue. In *Q* (2001), Quincy Jones refers to something Miles Davis said in *Miles* about Frances Taylor, whom Davis would marry: "He even wrote in his book that Brando and I were both in love with her, and that I even gave her an engagement ring. I told him, 'Miles, man, you know I never gave Frances no engagement ring.' He said, in that raspy voice of his, 'I know, Quincy, but the shit sounds good.'"[19]

The title page of *Q* lists no co-authors, but Jones thanks several collaborators in his acknowledgments, including one who created the book's "blueprint." Interspersed throughout the work are chapters written by others who have known Jones: brothers, childhood friends, wives, children, and fellow musicians. This multivoiced approach seems absolutely appropriate for the book's subject. Though a good performer, Jones is better known as an arranger, and *Q* is beautifully arranged. Jones's profound ambition, combined with his organizational skills, brought him enormous success as a producer as well. Besides being a jazz autobiography, *Q* belongs to the genre of mogul autobiography, that is, life stories written by wealthy, highly successful people, which has been so popular in American culture and which, of course, can trace its roots to Benjamin Franklin's autobiography.

FRAGMENTS OF THE SELF

The discovery of the molecular structure of DNA, which James D. Watson made with Francis Crick, Rosalind Franklin, and Maurice Wilkins, has proven to be a major contribution to modern science, but it was Watson's contribution to literature that popularized the image of the DNA molecule's elegant structure. *The Double Helix* (1968), Watson's autobiographical account of the discovery, proved a surprising best seller. The DNA molecule frightens even as it fascinates. The idea that this aesthetically beautiful molecule holds all the genetic material needed to determine individual identity calls to mind the closing lines of Robert Frost's sonnet "Design":

What but design of darkness to appall?
If design govern in a thing so small.[20]

The significance of the discovery only partly accounts for the popularity of *The Double Helix*. Much as Frederick Douglass manipulates the discursive strategies of popular literature, Watson uses techniques of the thriller, the detective story, and the gossip column to tell his story. A wunderkind who completed his doctorate at twenty-two, Watson went to Europe to do research. He observes, "It was certainly better to imagine myself becoming famous than maturing into a stifled academic who had never risked a thought."[21] Watson's intellectual snobbery simultaneously antagonizes readers and humanizes him. Regardless of his impressive scientific mind, he has the same faults and foibles as everyone else. *The Double Helix* is very much a story of personalities, the clash between ways of thinking and doing within the international community of scientists rushing to make a discovery they all knew would be momentous. Watson's narrative reflects the sheer excitement of intellectual inquiry.

Elizabeth Watson, James's sister, pops in and out of *The Double Helix*. In the final chapter, she is preparing to leave France to return to the United States, where she will marry. After shopping for a wedding present, brother and sister part ways but agree to meet later, for it was James's birthday. As his narrative ends, he explains: "I walked back across the Seine to our hotel near the Palais du Luxembourg. Later that night with Peter we would celebrate my birthday. But now I was alone, looking at the long-haired girls near St. Germain des Prés and knowing they were not for me. I was twenty-five and too old to be unusual."[22] Watson's conclusion reveals his fine sense of irony. One reviewer called his last sentence "one of the great 'camp' lines in modern prose."[23] At the factual level, his conclusion reminds readers that he made this extraordinary scientific discovery before he turned twenty-five. But the sentence also reasserts the story's personal intrigue. Watson, the co-discoverer of DNA, now understands how genetic material is transmitted through the process of reproduction. Concerning the complex social interactions that typically preface the act of reproduction, this nerdy young scientist has no clue. Imagining he knows what the young French women think about him, he reveals he has no idea what they are thinking. He may have discovered DNA, but he has yet to probe the mysteries of human existence.

The building blocks of personality go well beyond the chemical information encoded on the strands of DNA, as Theresa Hak Kyung Cha's *Dictee* (1982) reveals. Born in Busan during the Korean War, Cha emigrated to the United States with her family in the early sixties. She was educated in San Francisco, mastering French and studying art and literature. At Berkeley, she developed a passion for cinema, which motivated her to study at the Centre d'Études Américaines du Cinéma in Paris. She became a performance artist whose works combined live action and cinema. Incorporating different forms of expression, her stage performances anticipate *Dictee*. Cha relocated to New York in 1980, where she pursued her art at several levels. For a time, she worked for Tanam Press, a small independent publisher. In November

1982, a few weeks before *Dictee* appeared, Cha was murdered in Manhattan. She was thirty-one.

Publishing *Dictee* with Tanam Press, which published books on art, cinematic theory, literature, popular culture, and visual communication, Cha gave herself much more freedom than if she had tried to publish the work with a major commercial press. Tanam even published *Ktaadn*, a reprint of the "Ktaadn" chapter from Thoreau's *The Maine Woods*—an indication of that work's cutting-edge quality and ongoing impact. Cha draws upon film theory to assemble her book, combining various written texts in Chinese, English, French, and Korean with facsimiles of documents—some typewritten, others handwritten—and visual images: high-contrast photographic reproductions, black-and-white reproductions of paintings, and frame enlargements from the cinema. With its barrage of text and image *Dictee* seems weird, even scary, at first glance, but perhaps what Cha does is not so different from what Frederick Douglass does. Whereas Douglass's autobiography combines different forms of popular discourse, Cha's combines different kinds of verbal and visual information.

Beyond its startling visual appearance, the written text of *Dictee* presents problems in interpretation. As an autobiographer, Cha is notably reticent. She refrains from chronological personal narrative. Instead, she tells her story by presenting fragments of the lives of women who inspired her, from her mother to the Korean revolutionary Yu Guan Soon to Joan of Arc. Cha's challenging style recalls the prose poems of Baudelaire. Perhaps *Dictee* might make more sense if approached as poetry. Cha's solipsistic tendencies make her prose resemble the poetry of W. S. Merwin, whose allusions are highly personal, sometimes cryptic. Merwin's autobiographical writings are never so oblique. In *Summer Doorways* (2005), for example, he moves easily through time, embedding flashbacks within flashbacks, but never making it difficult to follow.

Like Watson, Cha tells a story about how building blocks of life are assembled to create identity. Unlike Watson's, Cha's story demonstrates that identity is constructed from many different factors beyond the chemical and biological. An eclectic mix of historical, cultural, political, and social factors contribute toward making Cha who she is. Her attempt to present these various factors, combined with her refusal to explain how they all interact, forces readers to make sense of the material. Cha's literary gem beautifully demonstrates how readers construct the identities of the autobiographers they read.

Chapter 4

Narrative Voice and the Short Story

FROM SKETCH TO SHORT STORY

The Sketchbook of Geoffrey Crayon (1819–20) forms a landmark in American literary history. Its date of publication is always given as two years because Washington Irving issued it in seven separate parts, starting in May of one year and continuing to September of the next. The year the first part appeared, 1819, traditionally divides early American literature from the next major literary period, the era of American Romanticism. Irving's book marks the transition. The main reason *The Sketchbook* starts a new literary period is because of two items contained within it, "Rip Van Winkle" and "The Legend of Sleepy Hollow." Though both can trace their roots to German folklore, these two can be considered the earliest short stories in American literature.

Like many books incorporating the word "sketch" in their titles, *The Sketchbook of Geoffrey Crayon* is essentially a book of travels. Most of its chapters are based on Irving's time in England. Writing in the persona of Geoffrey Crayon, a contemplative American bachelor, he gave himself the freedom to fictionalize when necessary and thus to enhance his personal story. That Irving was able to include two works of pure fiction set in America in this book of English travels indicates the desultory nature of its contents.

Irving reverted to an earlier persona for both "Rip Van Winkle" and "Sleepy Hollow": Diedrich Knickerbocker, the eccentric,

opinionated, scatterbrained scholar who narr
history, *The History of New York, from the Beginni*
End of the Dutch Dynasty (1809). A headnote tc
its manuscript survived among Knickerbock
but asserts that the original story derives from ...

The History of New York slyly lampoons the politics of Thomas
Jefferson and James Madison; "Rip Van Winkle" indicts the
Franklinian notions of hard work and stick-to-it-tiveness that
were lauded as essential aspects of the American national character. Instead of working hard to get ahead, Rip is a slacker who
prefers to loaf. He would rather go hunting than pursue more
gainful means of employment. He sleeps for twenty years and apparently ends up better off when he awakens. His son has grown
up, and his shrewish wife has died. Rip becomes the town sage
and influences the "rising generation."

After waking up, however, Rip briefly undergoes a crisis of identity. Upon seeing his son, who is his spitting image, he exclaims:

> I'm not myself—I'm somebody else—that's me yonder—
> no—that's somebody else got into my shoes—I was myself
> last night; but I fell asleep on the mountain—and they've
> changed my gun—and every thing's changed—and I'm
> changed—and I can't tell what's my name, or who I am![1]

The headnote to "Rip" calls the work a tale instead of a sketch,
a fact that shows how loose these generic labels used to be. During
the nineteenth century the word "sketch" would continue to be
used for travel literature, but "tale" would become the preferred
term for short pieces of fiction. The historical connotations of the
term "short story" have gone largely unnoticed, but the phrase
initially referred to children's tales. Not until the 1880s did it
come to have the meaning it has today.

Figure 4.1 *'Dis Von Don't Count': Mr. Joseph Jefferson, in His Celebrated Character of Rip Van Winkle*. Undated print. Library of Congress, Prints and Photographs Division (reproduction number LC-USZ62-5538).

A cluster of chapters in the *Sketchbook* concerns English traditions of celebrating Christmas. These sketches prompted a revival of Christmas celebrations in the United States. The association between Christmas and literature, in turn, prompted the emergence of giftbooks in the 1820s and 1830s. These hand-tooled, illustrated giftbooks, gilt-edged and calf-bound, proved an ideal literary venue and would remain so through the middle of the century. Containing a variety of sketches, poetry, and tales, the annuals offered a crucial outlet for contemporary authors, including Nathaniel Hawthorne and Edgar Allan Poe.

After disavowing *Fanshawe* (1828), his first novel, Hawthorne concentrated on short fiction, planning different collections of tales, which he hoped to link together with some sort of framing device. Hawthorne devoted much thought to possible collections before realizing that publishers disliked collections of stories because they sold poorly. Poe underwent a similar experience: he was unable to find a publisher for a planned collection of linked tales, which he intended to call *Tales of the Folio Club*.

Hawthorne destroyed many tales he had written but hesitated to abandon the genre. *The Token and Atlantic Souvenir*, a prominent Boston annual, published several of his early stories. *The Token for 1832*, for example, included two historical tales, "My Kinsman, Major Molineux," which shows what happens when a naive youth leaves the country for the city, and "Roger Malvin's Burial," in which Reuben Bourne abandons the mortally wounded Malvin in the woods, is subsequently racked with guilt, and must face the tragic consequences his action has for his family. In 1837, Samuel G. Goodrich, publisher of *The Token*, agreed to issue a collection of Hawthorne's stories as *Twice-Told Tales*. Goodrich published an expanded edition under the same title in 1842 and two other collections of Hawthorne stories, *Mosses from an Old Manse* (1846; expanded ed., 1854) and *The Snow-Image, and Other Twice-Told Tales* (1852).

Hawthorne's short fiction explores the depths of the soul and the intricacies of the past. Some stories are set in a past that anticipates the present, others in a present that cannot escape the past. "Young Goodman Brown" (1835), an allegory set in Puritan times, reveals what happens when a man leaves his wife, Faith, behind to attend a witches' coven. "The Minister's Black Veil" (1836) shows how a congregation reacts when their preacher, the Rev. Mr. Hooper, inexplicably covers his face with a veil. "The Birth-mark" (1843) tells the tale of a mad scientist's obsessive efforts to remove the birthmark from the face of his otherwise beautiful wife, Georgiana; "Rappaccini's Daughter" (1844) is another tale of a scientist's efforts to remake nature to suit himself and the tragedy that ensues. And "The Artist of the Beautiful" (1844) portrays the efforts of Owen Warland, a young watchmaker who attempts to create a beautiful object in the face of an insensitive public.

Using the third-person point of view, Hawthorne typically assumes an omniscient perspective. But he does not necessarily let his readers see the whole picture. As a literary stylist, he is at his best when he blurs the bounds between what happens in his stories and what his characters imagine is happening. Making their perception an integral part of his fiction, Hawthorne imbues his tales with psychological complexity.

The opening paragraph of "My Kinsman, Major Molineux" situates the story within its historical context, after which the narration shifts, bringing the reader into the action as Robin, the naive country-bred youth, enters town searching for his kinsman. The third-person narrator is omniscient, but the narration is often focalized from Robin's perspective. Robin's youth, his large physical stature, and his homespun clothing all mark him as a representative American naif. He visits the city at the invitation of his kinsman Major Molineux, the colonial governor. His arrival in town is reminiscent of Franklin's entry to Philadelphia in his *Autobiography* and foreshadows Pierre Glendinning's entrance to New York in Herman Melville's dark and daring novel *Pierre: or, The Ambiguities* (1852).

Robin asks everyone he meets to direct him to Molineux, but he is continually rebuffed. Lonely, he dreams of home, a mental image difficult to shake. "Am I here, or there?" Robin asks himself. This moment of existential uncertainty recalls what Rip Van Winkle says upon seeing his son. Whereas "Rip Van Winkle" challenges American attitudes toward success, however, "My Kinsman, Major Molineux" confirms them.

Robin finally sees the major, whom the townsfolk have tarred and feathered. He laughs aloud with them, his behavior symbolizing his break with his family and his acceptance in the community. Instead of returning home, Robin agrees to stay once a local man tells him: "You may rise in the world, without the help of your kinsman, Major Molineux."[2] The man's words echo promotion literature as they stress the opportunities for the individual to succeed in America without regard to family connections. The valorization of the individual is a long-standing American tradition: without it the whole enterprise would be unanchored.

POE AND THE FIRST-PERSON NARRATIVE

Unlike Hawthorne, Poe felt no compunction to use early American materials in his fiction. He took a more cosmopolitan approach. In his quest for literary originality, he invented new forms of fiction. "Murders in the Rue Morgue" (1841) is the first detective story in literary history. And "Hans Phaal" (1835) can be considered the first modern work of science fiction.[3] It could be said that Poe perfected the short story. The meticulous craftsmanship he applied to his early poetry he also brought to fiction. In a poem, according to Coleridge, every word counts. Poe went Coleridge one better. Not only does every word count, but so does the position of every word. Poe gave the genre of short fiction a new level of seriousness, creating tales gruesome in their imagery yet astonishing in their prescience.

Poe is best known as an author of gothic horror, but he never wanted to be pigeonholed. He sought to vary his writing as much as possible. Still, certain ideas, motifs, and patterns run across his fiction. He was fascinated with the extent to which people's exterior features could reflect their personality. Attire, decor, gait, handwriting, phrenology, physiognomy: Poe explored how all of these outward reflections of personality worked as legible signs, ways to understand the person behind them. Whereas the behavior of C. Auguste Dupin, the fictional detective Poe created for "Murders in the Rue Morgue" and reprised in "The Mystery of Marie Rogêt" (1843) and "The Purloined Letter" (1844), affirm the potential for reading such signs, "The Man of the Crowd" (1840) provides a more circumspect view, suggesting the essential illegibility of modern man. "William Wilson," which set the pattern for doppelgänger stories, conveys the duality of the self. Poe used the double motif in many other stories and many other ways. In "The Fall of the House of Usher," for instance, the narrator is a double for Roderick Usher, Roderick is a double for his twin sister, Madeline, and the house is a double for Roderick.

Whereas Hawthorne preferred the third-person point of view, Poe preferred the first. His innovative use of the first-person point of view may represent his most influential contribution to the history of narrative. He created narrators the like of which literature had never seen. The first-person voice naturally fosters a sense of emotional identification between narrator and reader. In Poe's stories, readers accept this relationship with mixed feelings of revulsion and fascination. "The Black Cat" (1843) is narrated by a man who has murdered his wife. The first-person narrative gives the tale a disturbing immediacy, as it provides an insider's view of the condemned murderer's mind. The coolness with which the narrator relates his tale only enhances the reader's uneasiness. We are privy to the machinations of a man who admits his mind is haunted by evil thoughts. He calmly relates how he killed his wife with an axe one day, methodically walled her up in his cellar, and afterward slept "soundly and tranquilly," unaware that he had also entombed their pet cat, still alive, inside the wall.

Melville used the short story to experiment with narrative point of view as well. In "Bartleby, the Scrivener" (1853), the narrator, an old, conservative Wall Street lawyer, takes his personal encounter with the mysterious Bartleby as an opportunity to tell a highly wrought tale. Instead of reporting Bartleby's story as a matter of fact, the narrator indulges his literary sensibilities and cultivates his sense of melancholy. Like "The Man of the Crowd," "Bartleby" occupies a transitional place in the history of American literature. Its somber tone and its emphasis on the mysterious unfathomability of human nature situate it in the Romantic period. But its urban setting—the realm of the lawyer and the financier—and its themes of loneliness, alienation, and determinism anticipate the realism of the late nineteenth century and the modernism of the twentieth.

VOICES OF THE OLD SOUTHWEST

The humorists of the Old Southwest date from the Romantic period but also anticipate realism. This loosely defined set of authors, stretching from Georgia to Arkansas, includes Augustus Baldwin Longstreet, Thomas Bangs Thorpe, and George Washington Harris.[4] The "scene" was their preferred genre, but many of their short works contain sufficient plot and character to make them full-fledged tales.

Georgia Scenes (1835) stands out as a classic of American humor, but Longstreet saw its composition as a documentary task. Though the plots of his stories are fictional, their details are fairly realistic. Longstreet purposely wrote them to record the behavior, folkways, mannerisms, and speech in Georgia during the early days of statehood. Three decades before realism would emerge as the dominant approach to fiction in American literature, Longstreet's tales exemplify its basic principles. His preface reads like a realist manifesto. Longstreet says of his "scenes": "They consist of nothing more than fanciful *combinations* of *real* incidents and characters; and throwing into those scenes, which would be otherwise dull and insipid, some personal incident or adventure of my own, real or imaginary, as it would best suit my purpose—usually *real*, but happening at different times and under different circumstances from those in which they are here represented."[5]

"The Horse Swap," a hilarious tale relating how one man took advantage of another in a trade, may be the most well-known story from *Georgia Scenes*, but others deserve attention, especially "The Fight," which tells the story of the top brawlers in one Georgia county, Billy Stallings and Bob Durham. Ransy Sniffle, a short, weaselly character who feeds "copiously upon red clay and black-berries," has been trying to foment conflict between these two, which comes about after their wives argue at the local millinery. Once Mrs. Durham calls Mrs. Stallings a "nasty, good-for-nothing, snaggle-toothed gaub of fat" there is no turning back.[6] As the fight approaches, Ransy Sniffle can scarcely contain his excitement. Once it begins, he and his fellow townsfolk are treated to a bloody scene accompanied by the loss of such minor appendages as one combatant's ear, the tip of the other's nose, and one finger.

Ransy Sniffle, the object of Longstreet's satire, represents the American spectator's macabre fascination with violence—yet he is not the only one. Through much of the story, the narrator seems like an omniscient third person, but during the heat of action, he interjects: "I looked, and saw that Bob had entirely lost his left ear and a large piece from his left cheek. His right eye was a little dis-colored, and the blood flowed profusely from his wounds."[7] The narrator, like Ransy Sniffle, belongs to the crowd who watch the fight. The violence intrigues him, too.

Indebted to both the oral tradition and the literary culture, "The Big Bear of Arkansas" (1841) is a short story of considerable sophistication.[8] Thomas Bangs Thorpe first published this tale in *The Spirit of the Times*, the sporting weekly edited by William T. Porter that consistently published top-notch humor. Intrigued with folk speech, Thorpe hesitated to give over his narrative completely to some loose-limbed, slack-jawed rustic. Consequently, he structured it as a frame tale, which allowed him to begin it in a voice not dissimilar to his own, that of an urbane southern gentleman, and then indulge his interest in folk speech partway through the story by handing the narrative reins over to Jim Doggett, a gregarious Arkansas bear hunter. The gentility of the outside narrator's voice thus frames the inside narrator's down-home twang. Thorpe's tale would exert a powerful influence on William Faulkner, who would write the other great bear-hunting story in American literature, "The Bear" (1942).[9]

George Washington Harris structured his Sut Lovingood stories as frame tales as well. Like Thorpe, Harris typically begins by speaking in the persona of a well-to-do southern gentleman but quickly lets his recurring inside narrator, Sut Lovingood, take over. In "Hen Baily's Reformation," which forms part of *Sut Lovingood: Yarns Spun by a "Nat'ral Born Durn'd Fool"* (1867), Sut describes the short story's title character as "a durn'd no-count, good, easy, good-fur-nuthin vagerbone, big es a hoss, an' lazy es a shingle-maker."[10] As this description suggests, Harris worked hard to present the nearly impenetrable dialect of the east Tennessee mountaineer. "Hen Baily's Reformation" shows what happens when a formerly jolly toper accidentally swallows a live lizard. A modern editor warns against spoiling the plot, so you must read for yourselves to learn about that lizard's circuitous peregrinations. You won't be disappointed.

Figure 4.2 Currier and Ives, *Bear Hunting*. Hand colored lithograph, undated. Library of Congress, Prints and Photographs Division (reproduction number LC-USZ62-33173).

CAPTURING THE WAY PEOPLE TALK

The humorists of the Old Southwest strongly influenced Mark Twain, the first major author of American literary realism. Their influence is apparent in both his novels and his short stories, including "The Notorious Jumping Frog of Calaveras County" (1865). Also structured as a frame tale, this story begins as its outside narrator reaches a California mining town in search of Simon Wheeler, the inside narrator who relates the story of Jim Smiley, a man who would bet on anything. Twain makes full use of the American storytelling tradition, incorporating multiple instances of tall talk and dark humor. Smiley's penchant for gambling leads him to train a frog for competition. Wheeler's story describes the time Smiley's frog finally lost. Instead of neatly tying up "The Notorious Jumping Frog" with a closing frame, Twain leaves it open-ended. The written story, he implies, presents only part of the tale-telling experience. As the printed word ends, the tale-telling tradition continues.

Charles W. Chesnutt shared a fascination with dialect and also used the frame tale structure to articulate it. "The Goophered Grapevine" forms the first story in *The Conjure Woman* (1899), Chesnutt's collection of dialect stories from rural North Carolina. The story begins in the voice of an educated, successful viticulturist from Ohio who travels to North Carolina looking for a vineyard to purchase. He meets Uncle Julius, a wily old man in the tradition of the African trickster hero who attempts to dissuade the Ohioan from purchasing the local vineyard because, he says, it is "goophered" or, in other words, conjured or bewitched. At this point Uncle Julius takes over the narration to relate to the would-be buyer how "Mars Dugal" hired a conjure woman to put a hex on his grapevines to prevent local residents from eating his grapes. Undeterred by Uncle Julius's tale, the outside narrator, as he explains in the closing frame, buys the vineyard and hires Uncle Julius as his coachman. After Uncle Julius's delightful inside narrative, however, the Ohioan's closing words fall flat.

Realist writers in the more genteel tradition hesitated to use dialect as extensively as Twain or Chesnutt, but they did use many other sophisticated narrative strategies in their short fiction. Sarah Orne Jewett, for instance, narrated "A White Heron" (1886) in the third person, but she varied her focalization, relating the story from the perspective of different characters as it progresses. Sometimes she speaks from the perspective of old Mrs. Tilley and other times from that of her granddaughter Sylvia or the young ornithologist who visits their isolated cabin searching for specimens. This narrative strategy is especially effective toward the end, when the story shifts to Sylvia's perspective as she decides to withhold her discovery of the heron's nest, depriving the ornithologist of his specimen and saving the heron's life.

NATURALISM AND THE SHORT STORY

Naturalism is realism without hope. Naturalistic stories typically depict desperate characters trapped by fate. American literary naturalism lends itself to longer works, such as Theodore Dreiser's *Sister Carrie* (1900) or David Graham Phillips's *Susan Lenox* (1917). The protagonists of such works are victims of environment, heredity, and pure chance. The novel gave naturalist authors room enough to express their bleak, deterministic outlook and to let their protagonists, and their readers, gradually feel the weight of the world clamping down on them. Two turn-of-the-century naturalist authors did excel in the short story: Stephen Crane and Jack London.

In *Green Hills of Africa* (1935), Ernest Hemingway calls "The Open Boat" (1897) one of Crane's two best short stories, the other being "The Blue Hotel."[11] Crane based "The Open Boat" on a life-threatening personal experience. He initially related the incident in a newspaper article, "Stephen Crane's Own Story," but realized the thrilling experience gave him the stuff for a fine short story and later recast his adventure as "The Open Boat." Crane changed the narrative point of view in the transfer from truth to fiction. "The Open Boat" flaunts its third-person, omniscient narration from the first paragraph, indeed, the first sentence: "None of them knew the color of the sky." With no formalities, the narrator insinuates himself into the heads of all of the lifeboat's nameless characters: captain, oiler, cook, and correspondent. The narrator knows what all four characters know and sees what they see.

Through his narrator, Crane created a sense of immediacy for his reader. Thinking about "The Open Boat," Ralph Ellison observed: "We become one with the men in the boat, who pit their skill and courage against the raging sea, living in their hope and despair and sharing the companionship won within the capricious hand of fate."[12]

The narrator reaches such a level of familiarity with conditions inside the lifeboat that he sometimes seems present. Other times he achieves an extraordinary distance, peering at the boat as if from on high. Yet other times he achieves distance from the men in the boat by revealing that he knows more than they do. Though the narrator possesses the ability to enter his characters' minds and read their thoughts, he does not always take advantage of this ability. Occasionally he prefers to let them articulate their thoughts themselves.

As the story progresses, the narrative becomes increasingly focalized from the correspondent's perspective, but Crane does not attribute all formulated thoughts to him. Many are the narrator's invention. That both the correspondent and the narrator are projections of Crane's self complicates matters further. Varying the narrative distance and changing the focalization, Crane creates a remarkable narrative that discursively replicates the story it tells. Telling a story of men stranded in the vast space of the ocean, Crane strands his readers within the space of his story, disorienting them as he tosses them to and fro, removing traditional narrative moorings and letting readers struggle toward comprehension.[13]

Personal experience helped shape many of Jack London's stories. Going to the Klondike in 1897 for the gold rush, he endured hazardous conditions that shaped his understanding of nature's severity and man's limitations when faced with that harshness. This dual theme is central to many of London's short stories. A prolific author, London wrote enough short stories to fill three

Figure 4.3 Bain News Service, *Jack London.* Photographic print. Library of Congress, Prints and Photographs Division (reproduction number LC-DIG-ggbain-00676).

thick volumes. "To Build a Fire," his most renowned tale, is narrated from an omniscient point of view. Unlike Crane's narrator in "The Open Boat," London's is more objective and less sympathetic. He presents the situation as a matter of fact, comparing man and beast. Human judgment is no match for canine intuition. Unable to build a fire at the end of the tale, the man perishes. His dog, which seeks shelter elsewhere, will live to see another day.

MODERN VOICES

The career of Ernest Hemingway marks a new phase in the history of the short story. Influenced by the naturalism of Crane and London, Hemingway stripped away all extraneous detail to create a lean writing style suitable for conveying the moral vacuity of modern existence, a mentality his audience received eagerly. Hemingway's highly readable prose veers from the intricate style characteristic of much modernist writing. His simple, declarative sentences have a soothing effect on the reader, providing oases of calm and clarity in a world of uncertainty. It is not Hemingway's sentences but the gaps between them that make his work modernist. Narrating his stories in as few words as possible, he forces readers to fill in those gaps and make sense of what is there as well as what is not.

Hemingway titled a major collection of his tales *The First Forty-Nine Stories* (1939). Almost any of the forty-nine could serve to demonstrate his narrative style. "A Pursuit Race" (1927), for one, embodies his long-standing interest in sport. This tale uses a cycling competition as a metaphor for the American odyssey of William Campbell, an advance promoter for a transcontinental burlesque show. Like a losing track cyclist in a pursuit race, Campbell gets caught by his frustrated pursuer, the show's manager, William Turner, who followed him from Pittsburgh to Kansas City. As short as it is, "A Pursuit Race" recapitulates the American journey west. Combined with a doppelgänger motif reminiscent of "William Wilson," the western journey no longer symbolizes an opportunity for escape or a chance to start a new life. Hemingway evokes the journey west to suggest instead the futility of trying to escape from the self.

Using dialogue to develop both plot and character, Hemingway often omits tag clauses identifying who says what. From their dialogue, it becomes clear that Campbell and Turner are close friends. As his employer, Turner should fire Campbell, who is no longer useful as an advance man. Despite a chronic drinking problem, Campbell managed to do his job, but now he has developed a heroin habit. Turner's tenderhearted sympathy for Campbell is touching. He leaves Campbell's hotel room, promising to return. After letting dialogue carry most of the tale, Hemingway delivers the conclusion in the voice of his omniscient, third-person narrator: "But when Mr. Turner came up to William Campbell's room at noon William Campbell was sleeping and as Mr. Turner was a man who knew what things in life were very valuable he did not wake him."[14] Given the futility of any kind of permanent escape, sleep provides temporary solace, a way to separate the self from all the problems, uncertainties, frustration, madness, evil, and darkness of everyday existence. Hemingway's sentiments are symptomatic of the times. W. C. Fields echoes them in *My Little Chickadee* (1940): "Sleep! The most beautiful experience in life. Except drink."

Like Hemingway, Richard Wright often develops character and plot through the use of dialogue, but the Mississippi-born Wright can trace his work to many antecedents in American literature, from the humorists of the Old Southwest to such realists as Charles Chesnutt. But Wright's daring innovations in narrative technique clearly mark his work as modern. "Almos' a Man" (1940) first appeared in *Harper's Bazaar* but was later retitled "The Man Who Was Almost a Man" when published in *Eight Men* (1961). The story begins with the following sentence: "Dave struck out across the fields, looking homeward through paling light."[15] In the second sentence, the narrative enters Dave's stream of consciousness. The remainder of the opening paragraph alternates between the narrator's third-person voice and Dave's internal monologue. Though potentially sophisticated, this narrative technique does pose special problems.

Speaking about Wright's narrative strategies in this story's opening paragraph, novelist Cecil Brown commented on the unknowability of Dave's thoughts: "We believe we know something about the boy's mind, but we can't be sure, for after all, it was *reported* to us by the narrator. We can never really know the boy."[16] Cecil Brown's literary criticism is fairly evenhanded, but he comes down hard on Wright in *The Life and Loves of Mr. Jiveass Nigger* (1969), a novel in the tradition of African trickster tales. In the pages of this picaresque novel, Brown finds the time to critique Bigger Thomas, the protagonist of Wright's *Native Son* (1940), characterizing him as a demoralized figure "who went through life living masochistic nightmares, who lived in fear of the Great White Man who in reality was a substitute for some psychic guilt."[17] George Washington, as Brown audaciously named the hero of *Life and Loves*, does not walk about with a chip on his shoulder. Instead, he uses his capacity for wordplay to empower himself, to get whatever he wants.

Figure 4.4 Carl Van Vechten, *Richard Wright*. Photographic print, gelatin silver, 23 June 1939. Library of Congress, Prints and Photographs Division, Carl Van Vechten Collection (reproduction number LC-USZ62-42502).

The climax of "The Man Who Was Almost a Man" comes when Dave accidentally shoots and kills a mule. The episode provides another instance of dark humor. When the townsfolk learn what has happened, they laugh at Dave. "Well, boy," one remarks, "looks like yuh done bought a dead mule!" The idea of buying a dead mule recalls the humor of "The Horse Swap," but explicit economic details make the story a modern indictment of capitalism. A Sears catalogue, after all, had fostered Dave's desire for a gun. Considering what that dead mule will cost him, Dave recognizes he must work for two years to pay for it: an unbearable thought. Instead, he hops a freight train out of town. The story's ending is ominously open-ended: "He felt his pocket; the gun was still there. Ahead the long rails were glinting in the moonlight, stretching away, away to somewhere, somewhere where he could be a man . . ."[18] The ellipsis dots, which are part of the story, leave Dave's fate a mystery. Where is he headed? How far will he go to prove his manhood? Will his sole possession, the gun, play a role?

Desire for possession also forms a theme of Flannery O'Connor's "Good Country People." One day an apparently innocent young Bible salesman named Manley Pointer appears at the home of the aptly named Mrs. Hopewell and her daughter, a hulking woman originally christened Joy who has changed her name to Hulga, the ugliest name she knew. With an artificial leg and a doctorate in philosophy, Hulga possesses a cynical outlook opposing her mother's homespun, cliché-driven optimism. O'Connor obviously enjoyed manipulating Mrs. Hopewell's characteristic sayings, often heaping one cornball saying atop another.

Convinced that Manley Pointer represents pure innocence, Hulga gets the idea to seduce him, regardless of her own lack of sexual experience. They meet in a hayloft, where he convinces her to show him how her leg attaches. Shocked at this intimate request, she interprets it as another sign of innocence and complies. Once her leg is detached, he pops it into his sample case and rushes off, telling her: "You ain't so smart. I been believing in nothing ever since I was born!"[19] Stealing her leg, Manley Pointer—not his real name, he admits—procures a trophy of his conquest. He once obtained a woman's glass eye similarly. Like Dave in "The Man Who Was Almost a Man," Hulga ends ups stranded and alone. Her future is easier to foretell. Eventually someone will discover her there, and she will have to explain to her mother how she lost her leg. At least one uncertainty remains: will Hulga admit that she was the true innocent in this drama, or will she keep hiding behind her mask of cynicism?

POSTMODERN VOICES

Many people bandy about the term "postmodernism" without knowing precisely what it means. When it comes to American literature, several factors distinguish postmodernism from modernism. Postmodernist fiction is generally more ironic and more allusive. Often its irony arises from its allusions. It alludes to high culture (Western art, classical music, great books) even as it simultaneously alludes to popular culture (comic books, jazz, television, movies). These mixed cultural references have the dual effect of bringing down high culture and elevating popular culture, of questioning the validity of such hierarchical distinctions.

Perhaps the phrase "discordant mix" may characterize postmodernist literature best. Not only do these works mix cultural allusions, but they also mix tone, combining audacious humor with profound seriousness. Mixed, too, are genre and style. Postmodernist literature often combines multiple genres, challenging the boundaries between them. A self-conscious playfulness frequently characterizes postmodernism. The style has proliferated for more than forty years in different media. Cha's *Dictee* is postmodernist autobiography; *Family Guy* is postmodernist television.

Thomas Pynchon's "Entropy" (1960) borrows a scientific concept, transforming it into a central tenet of his story. According to the idea of entropy, everything naturally tends toward disorder. What occurs in nature Pynchon applies to society, which he also sees as tending to disorder. Pynchon is not alone; other postmodernists have understood the concept's usefulness. William Gaddis, a prominent postmodern American novelist best known for his experimental satirical novel *The Recognitions* (1955), recently compared his career with Pynchon's, observing, "We both stumbled onto entropy as a core concept."[20]

Set in an apartment building in Washington, D.C., Pynchon's "Entropy" shifts between the downstairs apartment, where a character named Meatball Mulligan is hosting a marathon lease-breaking party, and upstairs, where Callisto lives. Gone is the restrained protagonist and all Hemingwayesque austerity; Pynchon riots in description. "Entropy" is rich with references to literature (Henry Adams, Djuna Barnes, William Faulkner, Henry Miller), music (Charles Mingus, Gerry Mulligan, Modest Mussorgsky), painting (Henri Rousseau), and science (Ludwig Boltzmann, Josiah Willard Gibbs, Claude Shannon).

The allusion to Claude Shannon occurs as two guests argue over communication theory. Here Pynchon presents an instance of postmodernist irony: he has his characters communicate about the difficulties of the communication process. Saul, one of the party guests, says that the word "love" in the sentence "I love you" is problematic because it creates noise. Saul observes, "Noise screws up your signal, makes for disorganization in the circuit."[21] His diction echoes Shannon's *Mathematical Theory of Communication* (1949), a classic of American scientific literature. Shannon's theory suits the theme of entropy: he discovered one way to find order in disorder. He discovered how to make the study of information flow subject to precise mathematical treatment. (Shannon coined the term "bit.") Practically speaking, his discovery let him embed one telephone conversation within the intermittent silences of another.

In Pynchon's story, the activities in the two apartments end in opposite ways. Downstairs, Meatball Mulligan consciously decides to prevent his party from deteriorating into total chaos and imposes some order on the situation. Upstairs, Callisto's hermetically sealed, climate-controlled apartment proves stifling. At last he breaks the window and awaits the time when his apartment will achieve equilibrium with the February night.

Given the richness of its allusions and the theme of entropy, the story takes on further irony when seen in terms of its narrative point of view. Since "Entropy" is narrated from the third person, all the clever allusions and references that occur outside the direct discourse emanate from the narrator. He is the one who is an expert on literature and music and painting and science. Telling a story about disorder, he is imposing his consciousness onto the narrative. Ironically, "Entropy" is a highly wrought, meticulously crafted story.

The same descriptors apply to the short fiction of Raymond Carver. After establishing himself with such story collections as *Will You Please Be Quiet, Please?* (1976) and *What We Talk About When We Talk About Love* (1981), Carver continued to expand the range of his short fiction. "Cathedral" marks a new development in his growth as an author. He often spoke of the story as a breakthrough work, one that allowed him more creative freedom than anything he previously had written. "Cathedral" is told by a first-person narrator who is bigoted and self-centered but quite funny. Contributing to the tale's complexity, Carver created a narrator with a deliberately goofy writing style who is not totally in control of his materials. The story relates a time when a blind man, whom the narrator's wife had previously known, comes to visit.

Jealous of his wife's attention to the blind man, the narrator deliberately refuses to name the man on one page, but then, a page or two later, accidentally lets slip his name, Robert: an indication of some slippage in his narrative control. Once Robert arrives, the narrator is flippant but still funny. Prompted by a television documentary, Robert asks him to draw a picture of a cathedral on some paper with enough texture that he could feel with his fingertips the lines his host would draw. As the narrator draws and Robert senses the texture of his drawing, the two talk and the evening becomes something special. Unexpectedly, the smart-alecky narrator undergoes an epiphany.

In recent decades, Sandra Cisneros has been one of the most outstanding authors of short fiction. In "Woman Hollering Creek" (1991), for instance, Cisneros tells the story of Cleófilas, a woman trapped in an abusive marriage. The narrative complexity belies the story's potentially mundane subject. The narrator seems to be a hybrid between first person and third person. She addresses readers like a close friend and says that she plans to attend Cleófilas's wedding early in the story but never really materializes as a character. Later in the story, she seems omniscient. But like Hawthorne's omniscient narrators, Cisneros's narrator feels no need to tell readers all she knows.

Cleófilas herself never takes over the narration, but sometimes the narrative is focalized from her perspective. Like Hemingway, Cisneros leaves out considerable explanatory detail and makes the story more powerful for it. Since much of the domestic violence is omitted, its fact becomes forceful as other characters in the story notice it. Pregnant, Cleófilas visits a clinic. Graciela, a woman who works at the clinic, calls Felice, a friend belonging to an informal women's help network. Graciela's description of Cleófilas is chilling: "This poor lady's got black-and-blue marks all over. I'm not kidding."[22] Nowhere else in the preceding story had Cisneros revealed the extent of the domestic abuse. Felice picks up Cleófilas and drives her to safety, a place where she can put her past behind her. Finally she's free. For the first time in a long time, she relaxes and laughs out loud.

Chapter 5

Poetry

EMILY DICKINSON AND WALT WHITMAN

Many consider Emily Dickinson and Walt Whitman the leading American poets of the nineteenth century. Yet two authors could hardly differ more in terms of style or temperament. Dickinson preferred to stay in her native Amherst, Massachusetts, to live and write in obscurity, to shield herself and her verse from all but the eyes of her family and a few sensitive friends. Whitman, alternatively, imposed himself upon the reading public, creating a larger-than-life persona that speaks to all. He built himself into his poems, becoming a vehicle to help readers see the world more deeply. "Song of Myself" is Whitman's fullest expression of his thoughts and feelings, but much of his verse embodies his philosophy of living. Together the private nature of Emily Dickinson and the public presence of Walt Whitman exemplify a paradigm that runs through the history of American poetry.

"Salut au Monde" reveals how Whitman uses his personal figure to demonstrate the universality of human brotherhood. "O take my hand Walt Whitman!": so the poem begins. Talking to himself, the poet is both leader and follower on this poetic journey. He encourages people to feel the humanity within the self. Deep personal understanding can broaden individual perspective, creating a sense of humanity large enough to include everyone. In the third stanza, the poet engages his sense of hearing, attuning himself to people from around the globe: "I hear the Arab muezzin calling from the top of the mosque, / I hear the Christian priests at the altars of their churches." In subsequent stanzas, the poet engages his sense of sight in a similar manner. At times he sees the entire world from afar, his field of vision encompassing the whole planet, "a great round wonder rolling through space." He sees the past, and he sees the future. Circling the globe, he salutes all men and women, encouraging them to embrace their shared humanity.[1]

Whitman published the first edition of his signature volume, *Leaves of Grass*, in 1855. After that, he kept revising, expanding, and republishing the book. "Salut au Monde" appeared in the 1856 edition and subsequently remained a part of the book. Whitman saw his ever-expanding work as an extension of the self. In his essay "A Backward Glance o'er Travel'd Roads," he called *Leaves of Grass* "my definitive *carte visite* to the coming generations of the New World."[2] In other words, the printed book was his way of introducing himself to the reading public, both readers of the present and those of the future.

Dickinson, on the other hand, kept her verse in manuscript. The few poems published in her lifetime appeared anonymously and apparently without permission. Instead of putting her verse in print, she copied out poems by hand and gathered these manuscripts together into fascicles, little handwritten booklets ideal for sharing privately with close friends.

Her desire for obscurity sometimes manifests itself in her verse. Consider the following poem:

> I'm Nobody! Who are you?
> Are you—Nobody—too?
> Then there's a pair of us!
> Don't tell! they'd banish us—you know!

Figure 5.1 Richard Halls, *Federal Dance Theatre Presents Salut au Monde: Adapted from a Poem of That Name by Walt Whitman.* Silkscreen print, 1937. Library of Congress, Prints and Photographs Division, Work Projects Administration Poster Collection (reproduction number LC-DIG-ppmsca-07144).

How dreary—to be—Somebody!
How public—like a Frog—
To tell your name—the livelong June—
To an admiring Bog![3]

Written around 1861, this poem satirizes the nascent cult of celebrity, which was partly influenced by the invention of photography and concomitant boom in steel-engraved portraiture derived from daguerreotypes.[4] Dickinson's poem parallels a remark Herman Melville made a decade earlier. Refusing to have his picture taken, Melville told Evert Duyckinck, "Almost everybody is having his 'mug' engraved nowadays; so that this test of distinction is getting to be reversed; and therefore, to see one's 'mug' in a magazine, is presumptive evidence that he's a nobody."[5] Like Melville, Dickinson satirized the superficial culture that linked personality and public identity.[6]

After identifying herself in negative terms in the opening line, the speaker of "I'm Nobody" expresses curiosity about the reader's identity, eagerly hoping they share the feeling of being nobody. The sense of camaraderie she articulates resembles that of the two kinsmen who "talked between the Rooms" in Dickinson's poem "I Died for Beauty—But Was Scarce." She urges the reader to keep their shared feelings secret, sensing that two nobodies might make a somebody and therefore elicit public curiosity. In one version of the poem, Dickinson wrote "advertise" in the fourth line instead of "banish us." Though these two alternatives may seem quite different, they had the same effect from Dickinson's viewpoint: an advertisement would embarrass her so much that she would be effectively banished from society.

In the second stanza, the speaker of the poem imagines what it might be like to be a somebody, which sounds pretty absurd. After using a traditional comparison—"like a Frog"—she sets up a startlingly original use of personification: "admiring Bog." Depicting the public as a bog, Dickinson emphasizes people's general ignorance and naïveté. To her, the public debased art. The process of publishing a creative work exposed it to an insensitive, uncaring audience whose only way of valuing art is to place a price tag on it. As Dickinson said elsewhere, "Publication—is the Auction / Of the Mind of Man."[7] The contrast between Emily Dickinson and Walt Whitman, between private and public, can be found in poetry from around the globe, of course, yet it seems absolutely vital to American poetry.

COLONIAL AMERICAN VERSE

Like Emily Dickinson, the seventeenth-century New England poet Anne Bradstreet wrote for herself and a small circle of friends and family. She, too, circulated copies of her work privately. One acquaintance took a manuscript volume of her collected verse and published it in London without her consent but with a pretentious title, *The Tenth Muse Lately Sprung Up in America* (1650), the first published book of verse by a woman in the English language. Initially shocked and dismayed, Bradstreet begrudgingly accepted the fact of publication, revised and expanded her collection, and republished an authoritative second edition in Boston many years later as *Several Poems Compiled with Great Variety of Wit and Learning Full of Delight* (1678).

"The Author to Her Book," which appears in the second edition, conveys Bradstreet's reaction to the first. It begins:

> Thou ill-form'd offspring of my feeble brain,
> Who after birth did'st by my side remain,
> Till snatcht from thence by friends, less wise than true,

Figure 5.2 *Governor Simon Bradstreet House*, 1667. Library of Congress, Historic American Buildings Survey (call number HABS MASS,5-ANDON,1–2).

> Who thee abroad, expos'd to publick view,
> Made thee in raggs, halting to th' press to trudg,
> Where errors were not lessened (all may judg).[8]

The book-as-child metaphor is not unusual. In "The Author to His Book," which prefaces his uproarious promotional tract *A Character of the Province of Maryland* (1666), George Alsop wrote, "I must lay double-clothes unto thy Bum, / Then lap thee warm, and to the world commit / The Bastard Off-spring of a New-born wit."[9] In her poem, Anne Bradstreet layered several metaphors atop the original one. She critiqued the book as "ill-formed" but, protective of it, became offended when the child was kidnapped, taken to England, and exposed to the public eye, which magnified its faults all the more.

The Rev. Edward Taylor, who is considered the foremost poet in the literary history of colonial New England, was more successful in keeping his verse from public view. Though Taylor created a huge body of poetry, he published just part of one poem in his lifetime, "Upon Wedlock, and Death of Children," which Cotton Mather included with his consolation sermon *Right Thoughts in Sad Hours* (1689). Taylor did not write solely for himself. He composed *Gods Determinations Touching the Elect*, a multipoem cycle, for his congregation in Westfield, Massachusetts. The work was not printed, but it did circulate in manuscript form. *Gods Determinations* had a didactic purpose: Taylor wrote it as an enjoyable way for his congregants to learn their catechism.

Preparatory Meditations, First and Second Series forms the basis for Taylor's lasting reputation. He wrote the individual poems that constitute this work solely for himself. They helped prepare him spiritually to administer the eucharist. Writing these private, meditative poems, he sought to understand the Holy Scripture more fully and bring himself closer to God. The only volume of English verse Taylor had in his library at the time of his death was the second edition of Bradstreet's poetry.[10] But his verse conveys his familiarity with seventeenth-century English poetry. Taylor's meditations are filled with elaborate metaphysical conceits: figures of speech that use wildly innovative comparisons to startle readers into new ways of thinking. Though his conceits are original, they do suggest the influence of such English poets as George Herbert.

In "Meditation Twenty-Nine," for instance, Taylor developed his conceit using the language of horticulture. Whereas God is "a golden Tree, / Whose Heart was All Divine," the speaker of the poem is "a Withred Twig, dri'de, fit to bee / A Chat Cast in thy fire." But if that dry twig can be grafted onto the golden tree, then it will blossom. In the fifth stanza, the poet suspends his lengthy horticultural metaphor for a series of brief metaphors cataloguing his relationship with God:

> I am thy Patient, Pupill, Servant, and
> Thy Sister, Mother, Doove, Spouse, Son, and Heire:
> Thou art my Priest, Physician, Prophet, King,
> Lord, Brother, Bridegroom, Father, Ev'rything.[11]

Expressing his relationship with God, Taylor understands that he's nobody, too. As a devout Christian, he willingly subsumes his personal identity within God's.

Though the poets of the colonial South found subjects for verse different from those of their New England counterparts, their work also manifests the public/private dichotomy. Colonial Virginia did not have a printing press until 1730. Before then, authors who wanted something printed had to send their manuscripts to London. Few local poets bothered. Instead, they circulated their verse privately. Even after William Parks established the first press in Williamsburg, many Virginia poets continued circulating their work in manuscript only.

The most versatile poets let their intended audiences determine whether they published a work. Colonial Virginia poet Robert Bolling, for instance, had a keen sense of audience. Poems intended for a cosmopolitan readership he sent to London to appear in such periodicals as *Imperial Magazine*, *London Magazine*, and *Universal Magazine*. Poems satirizing local people and events he published in the *Virginia Gazette*. And poems intended for fit, though few readers he circulated privately. Such is the case with his mock epic, "Neanthe," which survives in a manuscript volume, "A Collection of Diverting Anecdotes, Bon Mots and Other Trifling Pieces" (1764).

Keeping "Neanthe" private, Bolling gave himself the freedom
to write in a daring and audacious manner. "Neanthe" resembles
Ebenezer Cook's renowned mock epic *The Sot-Weed Factor* (1708)
(which would inspire John Barth's picaresque postmodern novel
The Sot-Weed Factor [1960]). Both Cook's poem and "Neanthe" are
patterned on Samuel Butler's *Hudibras* (1663). Cook filled his poem
with humorous situations, but "Neanthe" outdoes *The Sot-Weed
Factor* in terms of racy description and bawdy suggestiveness.

Bolling engaged the senses to describe the behavior and physical appearance of his eponymous hero:

> One Quality Neanthe had,
> Which almost ran her Lovers mad.
> A most divine and powerful Scent
> She scattered round, where e'er she went,
> Which, smelt by them, gave such keen Twitches,
> They scarce contain them in their Breeches.[12]

Two suitors vie for Neanthe's hand, Dolon and Euphenor, both
names recalling characters from Homer's *Iliad* and thus reinforc-
ing the poem's mock heroics. To settle their rivalry, Dolon and
Euphenor agree to a farting contest, but once Dolon cheats, the
two men resort to fisticuffs. Their rousing battle looks forward to
Longstreet's "The Fight."[13] After Euphenor accidentally kills
Dolon, Neanthe, who loved Dolon more, kills herself. The poem
ends with a mock elegy, which praises Neanthe's beauty and wit
and thus slyly critiques all elegiac verse. By no means is "Neanthe"
representative of early American poetry as a whole, but it fits well
within the humorous literary traditions of the South.

As colonial American newspapers proliferated in the run-up to
the Revolutionary War, so did the amount of published verse.[14]
Given the current political turmoil, much of the newspaper verse

was satirical, but early American poetry took many different forms: biblical paraphrase; character sketches; devotional poetry; elegy; topical verse on current events; occasional verse, such as poems celebrating the arrival of a new governor; literary quarrels carried out in rhyme; translations from the ancient classics; and versifications, which involved converting a preexisting prose text into poetry, usually with satirical intent. Political speeches given by the British colonial authorities were frequently versified, but early American poets recognized that they could versify almost any text. One of the most delightful works of Revolutionary Connecticut poet David Humphreys versifies a folktale: "The Monkey Who Shaved Himself and His Friends: A Fable." Several poems published in the early American newspapers even celebrate the printing press, an engine of enlightenment that would make ideas available to all.

OTHER MAJOR NINETEENTH-CENTURY POETS

The work of other major nineteenth-century American poets— Edgar Allan Poe, Herman Melville, Stephen Crane—suggests growing complexities in the relationship between poet and public. From the eighteenth century through the nineteenth, the number of newspapers increased exponentially. Since nearly every local paper had a poetry column, nearly all amateur poets who wished to publish their work could do so. While elite poets in colonial times kept their verse in manuscript, many who considered themselves serious poets in the nineteenth century recognized book publication as a way to distinguish their poetry from that of the newspaper poetasters. While still in his early teens, Poe understood that a published volume would be the best way to establish himself as a poet. At eighteen, he accomplished this goal with

Tamerlane and Other Poems (1827), closely followed by two more published collections, *Al Aaraaf, Tamerlane and Minor Poems* (1829) and *Poems* (1831).

From 1831, Poe concentrated on writing short stories, but he made a triumphant return to poetry a decade and a half later with the publication of "The Raven." The poem attracted the attention of Evert Duyckinck, who invited Poe to contribute a collection of his verse to the Library of American Books. *The Raven and Other Poems* (1845) included nearly all the poems from his earlier collections and those he had written since. This collection firmly established Poe's enduring reputation as a poet. For decades after his death in both the United States and Great Britain, Poe was more respected as a poet than as an author of weird tales.[15]

When Herman Melville turned from fiction to verse, he, too, saw a book-length collection as the way to establish his poetic reputation. Unable to find a publisher for his first collection in 1860, he did not achieve recognition as a poet until after the Civil War, when he published *Battle-Pieces and Aspects of War* (1866). The poems that constitute this collection of war poetry are unified by their subject matter and rough chronological organization. Melville's daring changes of voice and form add variety to the collection and, as its subtitle suggests, let him depict many different aspects of war.

"Donelson," which describes the South's surrender of Fort Donelson in Tennessee, is one of the most technically brilliant works in *Battle-Pieces*. Melville makes the act of reading in public a crucial motif of the poem. Several interested citizens have gathered around the bulletin board of a newspaper office during an icy rainstorm to read the latest telegraphic news reports. They publicly share the news. The poem alternates between the narrator's description of the crowd around the bulletin board and the news reports that depict the action at Fort Donelson.

Figure 5.3 Kurz and Allison, *Battle of Fort Donelson*. Lithograph, 1887. Library of Congress, Prints and Photographs Division (reproduction number LC-DIG-pga-01849).

Melville applies a technique in "Donelson" that would become known as crosscutting with the development of motion pictures. Much as a movie cuts between action taking place at two different locales, this poem alternates between battlefield and bulletin board. The close-up is another proto-cinematic technique Melville uses in "Donelson." After the crowd has dispersed, Melville inserts a poignant close-up of the handwritten news bulletin: "Washed by the storm till the paper grew / Every shade of a streaky blue, / That bulletin stood."[16] This close-up puts a period to what had come before and serves as a transition for what follows. In "Donelson," Melville combines sound and image to tell the story of the fall of Fort Donelson but also to depict the production of news during wartime.[17]

From the time *Battle-Pieces* appeared until the end of his life, Melville continued writing poetry. With the major exception of *Clarel* (1876), an epic account of a melancholy pilgrimage to the Holy Land, his verse remained in manuscript until the last few years of his life, when he published two brief collections, *John Marr and Other Sailors* (1888) and *Timoleon* (1891). Perhaps these collections should be characterized as printed, not published: Melville had twenty-five copies of each privately printed, which he distributed to close friends and relatives. These printed volumes were more like Emily Dickinson's manuscript fascicles than published volumes. Weary of unappreciative readers, Melville had long since abandoned hope of living off his writing. He now refused to compromise his aesthetic standards for the sake of sales. He, too, came to recognize publication as the auction of the mind of man.

Like Melville, Stephen Crane is better known for his fiction, but he published two collections of verse, *Black Riders* (1895) and *War Is Kind* (1899). The unique format his publisher chose for *Black Riders* enhances the modernity of Crane's verse. Individually quite short, the poems, in Amy Lowell's words, "spurted from the tip-top of the pages" and, therefore, left considerable white space toward the bottom.[18] Crane's publisher believed that the meaning of a text should help determine its physical appearance on the printed page. The poems in *Black Riders*, all printed in small caps, take the form of vignettes that occur in otherwise desolate space, the whiteness of the page reiterating the psychic vacancy of the verse.

Crane structured many of the individual works in this collection as dramatized encounters between the speaker of the poem and a solitary person he meets by chance. "In a Lonely Place" makes reference to a specific medium of mass communication:

IN A LONELY PLACE,

I ENCOUNTERED A SAGE

WHO SAT, ALL STILL,
REGARDING A NEWSPAPER.
HE ACCOSTED ME:
"SIR, WHAT IS THIS?"
THEN I SAW THAT I WAS GREATER,
AYE, GREATER THAN THIS SAGE.
I ANSWERED HIM AT ONCE,
"OLD, OLD MAN, IT IS THE WISDOM OF THE AGE."
THE SAGE LOOKED UPON ME WITH ADMIRATION.[19]

The opening prepositional phrase imparts a feeling of isolation, yet the old man's behavior—looking at a newspaper—reiterates an activity hundreds of thousands of people in Crane's New York engaged in every day. The lonely place the poet mentions is the heart of the city. People who open newspapers as soon as they take their seats on streetcars or park benches construct lonely places of their own, using the newspaper as a makeshift wall to isolate themselves from others. The poem's opening thus comments on the paradoxical nature of existence in the modern urban world. The crowded city is little more than a vast matrix of lonely places. The poem shows how the physical appearance of the printed page in *Black Riders* reinforces Crane's themes. Much as his poems appear as isolated texts amidst a vacant field of white, a newspaper held before the face in the modern urban world constitutes a printed text floating in space that turns people into abstractions.[20]

In Crane's day, as in our own, readers generally accepted what they read in the papers without question and let the mass media shape what they thought. In a poem included in his second collection of verse, *War Is Kind*, Crane characterizes the newspaper as, among other things, "a market / Where wisdom sells its freedom / And melons are crowned by the crowd."[21] Like those who read the

Boston Evening Transcript in T. S. Eliot's poem of the same name, Crane's newspaper readers generally "sway in the wind like a field of ripe corn."[22] The old sage of "In a Lonely Place," on the other hand, questions the meaning of the medium. Having never seen a newspaper before, he cannot discern its significance simply by looking at it. Instead, he must ask for clarification. The speaker exhibits an ironic self-satisfaction in the superiority he presumes over the old sage, who, paradoxically, seems more sagacious for his ignorance.[23]

MODERNIST VERSE

Several prominent modernist poets came from the West but ventured east to make their reputations. Born in Idaho, Ezra Pound came to Philadelphia with his family, eventually studying at the University of Pennsylvania, where he befriended William Carlos Williams and Hilda Doolittle (H.D.). Pound left America for Europe in 1908 and initially settled in London. Born in St. Louis, T. S. Eliot often visited Boston as a child. His family's close ties to New England effectively prevented him from identifying with his birthplace—though in "The Dry Salvages," which forms part of *Four Quartets* (1943), he does call the Mississippi River "a strong brown god—sullen, untamed, and intractable."[24] Eliot himself fled the New World for the Old, settling in London, where he met Pound and established his lasting reputation with *The Wasteland* (1922), which Pound helped revise.[25]

The list goes on. Born in San Francisco, Robert Frost moved with his family to New Hampshire. Though he would become an icon of American literature in his old age, he went to England as a young man to establish his career. Here he published his first two collections of verse: *A Boy's Will* (1913), which, in Pound's words, "has the tang of the New Hampshire woods," and *North of Boston* (1914), which includes such memorable works as "Mending Wall" and "After Apple-Picking."[26] Langston Hughes was born in Joplin, Missouri, and raised in Lawrence, Kansas, but he came to New York and later sailed to France. Staying in Paris for five months in 1924, he read the tales of Guy de Maupassant in French, which sparked his desire to become a writer. He returned to New York, where he became a leader of the Harlem Renaissance.

A general survey of Ezra Pound's career indicates the different directions the modernist poets took. In London, Pound became the center of a new and exciting movement. When H.D. arrived in 1911, she joined him and a number of British poets to found Imagism, a lean, visual style of writing poetry. According to the dictates the Imagists established, no extraneous words were allowed, nothing superfluous, nothing that does not contribute to a poem's effect. Though the Imagists saw themselves as doing something totally new, their aesthetic principles recall those of Dickinson, Poe, and Crane.

Pound's "In a Station of the Metro" (1913) may be the best-known Imagistic poem. Like "Donelson," the public space forms the setting for this poem. Unlike "Donelson," the communication process holds no place in this poem, which describes the images that people's faces cast on the windows of a passing subway train. Not only have people lost their individuality, but they have lost their corporeality as well. Each face is framed by the window and therefore isolated from every other one. Like Stephen Crane before him, Pound depicts the public as a matrix of lonely, private spaces.

Imagism played itself out quickly. By the time Amy Lowell reached London and claimed Imagism for herself, Pound was already heading in a different direction. He disliked the way she took Imagism—"Amy-gism," he called it. Pound moved to Paris in

1921, relocating to Italy a few years later. In the early 1920s he began what would be his life's work, *The Cantos*, which were published in successive groups from *A Draft of XVI Cantos* (1925) to *Drafts and Fragments of Cantos CX–CXVII* (1969).

In terms of American literary history, the impulse to create a long poem that encapsulated the nation extended as far back as Joel Barlow's patriotic *Vision of Columbus* (1787). Numerous other American poets had attempted long poems of their own. From Whitman's "Song of Myself" and Melville's *Clarel* in the nineteenth century, the impulse continued into the twentieth with Hart Crane's *The Bridge* (1930), William Carlos Williams's *Paterson* (1946–58), Charles Olson's *Maximus Poems* (1960–75), and John Berryman's *Dream Songs* (1969).

Pound saw the entirety of the literary past as fair game for him to appropriate for *The Cantos*. He took snippets from traditional Provençal ballads, classical Greek and Roman verse, and American political history. He even incorporated Chinese ideograms. *The Cantos* is large; it contains a multitude of images and ideas, thoughts and feelings, dactyls and diatribes. The work is so large—over eight hundred pages in the final collected edition—that it is often difficult to get a handle on the whole.

In Canto XXXI, the first item in *Eleven New Cantos* (1934), Pound took a new direction by incorporating passages from the correspondence of Thomas Jefferson and John Adams, which itself represents an enduring contribution to American literature. The letters of Jefferson and Adams that Pound excerpts stretch from the 1780s through the 1810s and concern subjects ranging from the creation of an American canal system to animosity toward monarchy, European ignorance of American history, memories of Benjamin Franklin, moral philosophy, pre-Revolutionary committees of correspondence, and much else. This canto suggests that private manuscripts of the past deserve public recognition in the present. The thoughts that one great mind shared with another not only are significant for their ideas but also form building blocks for modernist poets, who claim the right to appropriate whatever texts they wish, public or private, to express their own ideas and create their art.

THE END OF A PARADIGM

In the modernist era, the private/public paradigm in American poetry broke down. Perhaps the break began with Wallace Stevens. His poems are often enigmatic, but their cryptic quality is part of the meaning. Whereas earlier poets wrote manuscript poems for a few close friends or public poems for a wider reader-ship, Stevens wrote private poems for the public. His point is that private poems are the only ones a poet can really write. Everyone has a different way of viewing the world, but every once in a while the way two people view the world coincides. Stevens relishes such coincidences, moments when his mind and his reader's come together in shared thought.

"Thirteen Ways of Looking at a Blackbird" (1917) provides a good starting point for understanding Stevens's perspective, though it also complicates matters further. Not only does every-one have a different way of seeing the world, but each individual has many different ways of seeing things. Consisting of short, irregular stanzas, the poem reads like a series of Imagist poems all strung together. Providing thirteen variations on the same motif, it suggests many different ways one person can view the same subject. The ninth stanza provides a key for understanding Stevens's perspective:

> When the blackbird flew out of sight,
> It marked the edge
> Of one of many circles.[27]

According to this stanza's controlling image, every individual is surrounded by a circle, the radius of which equals the length of that person's line of sight. If two people are close enough to each other, then their circles may overlap. In other words, shortly before the blackbird flies from the first person's circle, it enters the second person's. For the briefest of moments, the two people see the same blackbird. The comprehensibility of Stevens's poetry depends on these brief overlaps. Many readers find Stevens's ideas puzzling, but his work exudes confidence, the confidence that his ideal readers will know what he means and share his insight.

Another poem may make this notion easier to comprehend. "The House Was Quiet and the World Was Calm" beautifully describes the process of reading a book late one summer night. Whereas the ninth stanza of "Thirteen Ways of Looking at a Blackbird" demarcates one circle, leaving the others implicit, this poem captures a moment when two circles, the author's and the reader's, overlap. The author articulates something that the reader has personally intuited but never expressed. Through the process of reading, the reader recognizes the author as a kindred spirit, someone who knows the same things, thinks the same ideas, sees the world the same way. During these rare, shared moments, the materiality of the printed page almost disappears: "The words were spoken as if there was no book." Closely identifying with the author, the reader is willing to dedicate himself or herself to the author, "to be / The scholar to whom his book is true." The reader hesitates to change position in any way, to move at all. Sharing an intensely pleasurable moment with the author, the reader wants nothing to disturb it. The calmness of the night is essential to the appreciation, "part of the meaning, part of the mind, the access of perfection to the page."[28]

Sylvia Plath, like Wallace Stevens, wrote private poems that appealed to a public readership. Unlike Stevens, she did not wrap her personal feelings and experiences in enigma. Instead, she took intimate autobiographical details and used them to construct a compelling personal mythology. When the speaker of "Lady Lazarus" (1962) talks about trying to kill herself every ten years or so, she is reflecting facts in Plath's troubled life. And when the speaker of "Daddy" mentions her father's "one grey toe / Big as a Frisco seal," she indicates another biographical fact. Otto Plath's diabetes had turned his toe gangrenous, and he died after an emergency leg amputation. His death haunted his daughter for the rest of her life. Though written as an allegory of a daughter renouncing her Nazi father, "Daddy" contains other autobiographical details, including her father's German origins and her first suicide attempt. The profound anger the speaker of the poem expresses toward her father, according to the prevalent interpretation, reflects Plath's own attitude toward her absent father. The poem ends uncomfortably: "Daddy, daddy, you bastard, I'm through."[29]

Yet even with all these personal references, "Daddy" participates in a discourse that has been a central part of American literature since Captain John Smith, namely, the effort to repudiate the parents—sometimes figured as the mother instead of the father—and establish an identity separate from the one foisted upon a person by birth. Traditionally, American authors repudiated the Old World for the New. Plath's critique of her father's German origins follows this tradition, yet, oddly, he personifies North America as well, with his toe as big as a San Francisco seal and "a head in the freakish Atlantic." To borrow a conceit from T. S. Eliot, Daddy lies across the continent "like a patient etherised upon a table." Repudiating her father, whom she associates with both Old World and New, the speaker of "Daddy" leaves herself nowhere to turn. These feelings, too, seem to reflect biographical fact. Through much of her life Sylvia Plath was beset by crippling depression. She felt helplessly trapped in this world and, on February 11, 1963, took her own life.

THE PRIVATE POET

The death of Sylvia Plath did not sound the death knell of the American poet. Far from it. The numerous creative writing programs established at colleges and universities across the nation over the past sixty years have permitted poets to flourish. Take Richard Hugo, for example. Hugo was a veteran of the Army Air Corps and a decorated war hero who returned from Europe to finish his education on the G.I. Bill. He enrolled at the University of Washington, studying under Theodore Roethke, then near the peak of his powers as both poet and teacher, "probably the best poetry-writing teacher ever," Hugo said.[30] After earning his B.A. in 1948 and his M.A. in 1952, Hugo took a position as a technical writer with Boeing, but the strength of his first book of verse, *A Run of Jacks* (1961), helped him secure a teaching position at the University of Montana, where he, in turn, flourished as both poet and teacher.

The title of *The Triggering Town* (1979), a selection of Hugo's classroom lectures, reflects his poetic method. Often the sight of a small, run-down western town would trigger his imagination and form the basis for a new poem. Hugo is the poet of small-town America. His verse captures the look and feel of these fast-disappearing places before the cities draw off their population and nature reclaims the rest.

In one lecture, Hugo identifies himself as a private poet, not in the sense of Anne Bradstreet, that is, a poet who writes for the self and a few close friends, but more like Wallace Stevens, someone whose published poems have a private nature. In Hugo's view, what separates the private poet from the public one is the way each uses language. "With the public poet the intellectual and emotional contents of the words are the same for the reader as for the writer," he explains. But with the private poet, "the words, at least certain key words, mean something to the poet they don't mean to the reader. A sensitive reader perceives this relation of poet to word and in a way that relation—the strange way the poet emotionally possesses his vocabulary—is one of the mysteries and preservative forces of the art."[31]

Given the private nature of much recent American verse, poets sometimes have difficulty finding sensitive readers who can understand them. Many readers are poets themselves, who often feel they need to express their appreciation in verse. Gibbons Ruark, who spent his career writing and teaching poetry at the University of Delaware before returning to his native North Carolina, wrote a poem for Hugo he titled "Drinking Wine with a Map of Montana." Written in the form of a verse epistle, this poem pays homage to Hugo's work. For the lonely speaker of Ruark's poem, the map of Montana is a drinking companion, a surrogate and stand-in for the poet whose work he enjoys but whom he has never met. That he can identify on a map places he knows only from Hugo's poetry assuages his loneliness and assures him that there is another poet out there whom he understands and, maybe, who might understand him.

Ruark first published "Drinking Wine with a Map of Montana" in 1976 and subsequently included it in *Reeds* (1978), a collection containing other poems addressed to poets—Michael Heffernan, Denise Levertov, James Wright. Other recent American poets have felt compelled to address poems to their peers. Richard Hugo himself wrote numerous verse epistles to other poets, which he collected as *31 Letters and 13 Dreams* (1977). In addition to Levertov and Wright, this collection addresses poems to several other prominent contemporary poets, including A. R. Ammons, Robert Bly, Charles Simic, and Gary Snyder.

The best American poets of the twentieth century, Hugo asserts, are all private poets, those who write verse without trying to communicate with their readers. In his advice to would-be poets, he recommends, "Never worry about the reader, what the reader can understand."[32] Yet his verse epistles, as well as Ruark's and those of many other contemporary poets, suggest a profound need to communicate, to let other poets know he understands them and express the hope that the others will reciprocate and convey their understanding. Emily Dickinson's question, "Are you—Nobody—too?" reverberates throughout the history of American poetry.

Chapter 6

The Drama of the Everyday

REPRESENTATIVE AMERICAN PLAYS

When Arthur Hobson Quinn published *Representative American Plays* in 1917, it formed the fullest anthology of American drama then available. While the collection remains a major contribution to the study of dramatic literature, it also reflects the sorry state of the American stage before the twentieth century. The anthology opens with Thomas Godfrey's tragedy *The Prince of Parthia* (1767). Notable as the first professionally produced play by an American author, *The Prince of Parthia* has little else to recommend it. Quinn's next selection, Royall Tyler's comedy *The Contrast* (1787), is memorable for the character of Jonathan, the stereotypical Yankee that would become a standard onstage and in political cartoons, but the plot is unoriginal: it derives from a popular British drama, Richard Brinsley Sheridan's *School for Scandal* (1777). Quinn included plays from many different genres: historical tragedy, a Pocahontas play (one of numerous Indian plays that dominated the American stage in the early nineteenth century), literary adaptation, melodrama, romantic comedy, romantic tragedy, and social comedy.

Most of Quinn's plays are hardly worth mentioning by name. A few are. Julia Ward Howe's *Leonora* (1857), a tragedy depicting a woman unable to kill her betrayer who kills herself, premiered five years before Howe established a lasting reputation as a songwriter with "Battle Hymn of the Republic" (1862). Dion Boucicault's *The Octoroon; or, Life in Louisiana* (1859) holds interest as a cultural artifact: it presents the story of a young biracial woman doomed by the love of her white slave master. David Belasco contributed to the history of the American stage by bringing a new level of realism to it. Quinn reprinted Belasco's *Madame Butterfly* (1900), which capitalized on the current fad for all things Japanese but is more notable because Puccini transformed it into an opera. Rachel Crothers's *He and She* (1911) dramatizes the tensions of the emerging feminist movement as it shows the problems resulting when a sculptor-wife wins a prize over her sculptor-husband.

Literary adaptations were among the most popular works on the nineteenth-century American stage. Quinn chose Joseph Jefferson's *Rip Van Winkle* (1866) to represent the genre. This stage version of Washington Irving's short story was second in popularity to the dramatizations of Harriet Beecher Stowe's *Uncle Tom's Cabin* (1852). Before the Civil War, dozens of theater companies crisscrossed the nation enacting *Uncle Tom's Cabin*. These "Tom shows" stayed popular for decades after the Civil War. They effectively transformed Stowe's muscular protagonist into the "Uncle Tom" stereotype, an old black man hated because he grovels before whites.

Designed for classroom use, *Representative American Plays* went through a second edition, several reprintings, and, in 1925, a revised and expanded third edition, which contains *Beyond the Horizon* (1920), a drama by a promising new playwright named Eugene O'Neill. Contrasted with the maudlin sentimentalism and stale clichés of the other plays, *Beyond the Horizon* showed much promise for the American stage. George Jean Nathan, the day's leading theater critic, called it "a hope and tonic to the American drama."[1] In this play and others, O'Neill took everyday scenes and settings, characters, and plots and imbued them with almost mythic significance, something other major American playwrights of the twentieth century would do as well.

Figure 6.1 *Palmer's Uncle Tom's Cabin Co.* Lithograph, 1899. Library of Congress, Prints and Photographs Division (reproduction number LC-USZ6-474).

EUGENE O'NEILL

Beyond the Horizon begins as two brothers, Robert and Andrew Mayo, meet along a country highway. A restless dreamer, Robert is curious to learn what lies beyond the horizon; Andrew, a hard-working pragmatist, is happy to stay put and till the soil like their father before them. Despite the brothers' contrary impulses, they understand each other. Andrew recognizes the trip will make Robert a "new man"; Robert appreciates that Andrew is wedded to the soil. As they talk, Ruth, the pretty woman who lives next door, joins them. Andrew is engaged to Ruth, but Robert is secretly in love with her—and she with him. When they confess their love, Robert disastrously stays behind to marry Ruth and till the soil while Andrew takes the voyage Robert had been planning.

Andrew's return visits, each separated by years, structure the remainder of the play. Every time he returns, he sees that his brother's farm, marriage, and health have worsened. Given Robert's incompetence as a farmer, Ruth regrets sacrificing Andrew for him and hurtfully tells Robert so. Andrew's last visit finds his brother near death, which now offers his only path beyond the horizon. Once Robert dies, Andrew castigates Ruth for her spiteful behavior and blames her for Robert's death. The drama ends with Ruth hurt and Andrew regretting his harsh words. *Beyond the Horizon* achieves a rare synthesis. O'Neill took a naturalistic plot—the story of a man fated to disaster because he sacrifices his personal dream to marry the woman he loves—and gave it a sense of tragic grandeur.

O'Neill would continue to give his dramas a visceral punch that transcends their commonplace settings and characters. Set in Johnny-the-Priest's saloon and on a coal barge, *Anna Christie* (1921) tells the story of Captain Chris Christopherson and his daughter, Anna. To protect her from "that ole davil sea," Chris had placed Anna on a farm in the Midwest, little realizing the sexual abuse she would encounter there. Unbeknownst to her father, Anna had run away from the farm and desperately turned to prostitution. As the play begins, she is coming to New York to see him.

Anna's first line, which occurs as she seats herself in the saloon, marks her as someone completely different from earlier women in American literature, the dainty, refined angels that populate the sentimental novels of the nineteenth century. "Gimme a whiskey—ginger ale on the side. And don't be stingy, baby," Anna calls to the bartender.[2] (The role of Anna Christie was Greta Garbo's first speaking role in motion pictures, so these words also constitute the first words that millions of moviegoers heard Garbo speak in her distinctive low purr.) Anna soon joins her father on the barge. One night they rescue four men from an open boat—perhaps an homage to Stephen Crane. One of the men, Mat Burke, falls in love with Anna and she with him. Chris dislikes the idea of Anna marrying a sailor, and he and Mat come to blows. To end the dispute, Anna tells both father and lover about her past. Initially, Mat leaves her, but remarkably he returns, forgives Anna, and agrees to marry.

Prostitutes in previous works of American literature typically meet tragic ends. In Stephen Crane's first novel, *Maggie: A Girl of the Streets* (1893), Maggie Johnson turns to prostitution after being seduced and abandoned but finally drowns herself. The few prostitutes allowed to survive are denied any kind of earthly happiness. In Harriet Beecher Stowe's *We and Our Neighbors* (1875), a secondary character named Maggie turns to prostitution. Though she reforms, Stowe refuses to let her marry or even enter conventional society. The title character of David Graham Phillips's *Susan Lenox* (also brought to the cinema by Greta Garbo) survives her time as a prostitute to become wealthy, but she never achieves happiness or personal fulfillment. Not until *Anna Christie* is the prostitute allowed to meet a man who forgives her past and agrees to marriage and with it the promise of a family and community acceptance.[3]

The words Anna speaks as she stands up to both Chris and Mat are inspiring: "But nobody owns me, see?—'cepting myself. I'll do what I please and no man, I don't give a hoot who he is, can tell me what to do! I ain't asking either of you for a living. I can make it myself—one way or other. I'm my own boss. So put that in your pipe and smoke it!" The words Mat speaks upon his return reinforce Anna's sentiments and indicate a major shift in the portrayal of women in American literature: "For I've a power of strength in me to lead men the way I want, and women, too, maybe, and I'm thinking I'd change you to a new woman entirely, so I'd never know, or you either, what kind of woman you'd been in the past at all."[4]

The idea of becoming a new man long had been part of the American literary discourse and would remain a recurring motif in O'Neill's work, but it seldom had been applied to women, who were held to much more rigid standards regarding their past behavior. Now, finally, a woman could escape her past, remake herself, and discover a new identity. *Anna Christie* did not change attitudes instantly, of course. In Robert Sherwood's drama *Waterloo Bridge* (1930) Myra turns to prostitution in wartime and also meets a tragic end. But *Anna Christie* did point the way toward a more open-minded portrayal of women in literature, one that included their growth as characters.

O'Neill would continue to exploit his ability to attribute mythic significance to the quotidian. In the coming years, he devoted himself to long, multiplay cycles, including the trilogy *Mourning Becomes Electra* (1931). Later that decade he began a project with an epic scope, *A Tale of Possessors Self-Dispossessed*, an eleven-play cycle regarding the failure of the American dream that would trace the history of two families from the Revolutionary War to the present day. This play cycle proved too ambitious even for O'Neill, who left it unfinished. He returned to the waterfront saloon for inspiration in *The Iceman Cometh* (1946), which can also be seen as a comment on the failure of the American dream and which inspired other saloon dramas including Charles Gordone's *No Place to Be Somebody* (1969).

O'Neill's title may initially seem strange, but it encapsulates the play's complexities. *The Iceman Cometh* takes place at Harry Hope's bar on Manhattan's Lower West Side. As Harry's birthday approaches, the barflies anticipate the arrival of Theodore Hickman or "Hickey," a hardware salesman who typically treats them to as much rotgut as they can swill. Hickey always retells a humorous story about an affair between his wife and the iceman. So O'Neill's title refers to the iceman of Hickey's tale but also to Hickey himself, the man who tells the iceman story.

When Hickey arrives toward the end of the long first act, he is completely different from the way the regulars remember him. He is sober, for one thing, and he has a mission: to disabuse them of the hopeless dreams that have sustained them through their downward spiral into poverty and alcoholism. Hickey continually calls their unrealistic hopes "pipe dreams," a proverbial phrase coined in the late nineteenth century that refers to visions experienced while smoking opium. Having abandoned his own hopes, Hickey feels renewed. "I'm like a new man," he says. Larry, the philosopher of the group, someone who continually rails against the others, seems content to bide his time until life runs its course. Hickey tries to convince Larry that he is not as aloof as he pretends, telling him he is as guilty as the others: "Waiting for the Big Sleep stuff is a pipe dream."[5]

Throughout his work, O'Neill sought to write how people really talked, and he used numerous proverbs and colloquialisms in his writing. The speeches of Hickey and the other barflies in *The Iceman Cometh* indicate O'Neill's use of language. Raymond Chandler, the author of *The Big Sleep* (1939), a sharp-edged, hard-boiled crime novel, took issue with one particular phrase, however. Privately critiquing *The Iceman Cometh*, Chandler observed, "O'Neill uses the expression 'the big sleep' as a synonym for death. He is apparently under the impression that this is a current underworld or half-world usage, whereas it is a pure invention on my part."[6]

Hickey's words convince many of the barflies to sober up, leave the bar, and pursue their dreams. A pessimist by nature, he assumes they will return disillusioned, but he also believes that they will be at peace with themselves at last. Larry remains unconvinced. He compares Hickey to the "Iceman of Death." The comparison is prescient: Hickey *has* murdered his wife. His joke about the iceman was a lie. His wife was faithful to him; Hickey was the one who cheated, but she continually forgave his infidelities. Her boundless goodness gave him an overwhelming sense of guilt, which he could suppress only by killing her.

Sure enough, the barflies return, having failed to live out their dreams, but unlike Hickey they do not achieve peace. They try to get drunk, but even the old reliable booze has no effect. They soberly listen as he explains why he murdered his wife. Hickey's calm, careful narrative is reminiscent of "The Black Cat." They gradually realize that they took the advice of a madman. Once the police arrest Hickey, all the others can get drunk again—all, that is, save Larry and Don Parritt, the son of one of Larry's former lovers. Throughout the play Parritt had seen himself as a parallel character to Hickey. He, too, is racked with guilt: he turned in his mother, a domestic terrorist, to the police. Parritt seeks Larry's sympathy, but Larry shoves him away. As the rest drink and sing, Parritt climbs to the top of the building and jumps off. Larry, the only one who notices, is shaken. The Iceman of Death will come for them all, but as the play ends, this sad little group seems content to get drunk and reconstitute their dreams. Like so much of his work, *The Iceman Cometh* is depressing, but O'Neill's ability to record the frailty, the vulnerability, the capacity for self-delusion everyone shares keeps audiences in thrall.

ARTHUR MILLER

First produced three years after *The Iceman Cometh*, *Death of a Salesman* (1949)—Arthur Miller's masterpiece—reinforces the significance of the salesman as a major figure in American culture. The salesman is a purveyor of dreams, one who transmutes a buyer's worldly success into material goods, those things that provide comfort yet which also serve as tangible symbols of that success. Not only does the salesman help others manifest their dreams, but he personally symbolizes the American dream through his own success. Willy Loman, Miller's tragic hero, had idolized salesmen in his youth. He became one to share their exalted, though representative, American status.

Loman uses the phrase that forms the play's title as he describes Dave Singleman, a highly successful salesman who had traveled around the country selling goods until his death: "When he died—and by the way he died the death of a salesman, in his green velvet slippers in the smoker of the New York, New Haven and Hartford, going into Boston—when he died, hundreds of salesmen and buyers were at his funeral."[7] Loman's depiction of Singleman's death establishes an ironic counterpoint for his own. Now sixty-three, Loman can no longer sell enough to support his family. He is one payment away from paying off a twenty-five-year mortgage—a major accomplishment, as his wife, Linda, observes. All the other material goods Loman has surrounded himself with are falling apart even before they are paid for, however. Willy Loman has some of the exterior trappings of one who has achieved the American dream, but when it comes to the emotional and spiritual fulfillment that ought to accompany success, he is sadly wanting.

Set during Loman's last twenty-four hours, *Death of a Salesman* contains a number of scenes depicting earlier moments in his life. Though influenced by the cinema, Miller hesitated to call these scenes flashbacks. He wanted to make the point that different moments in a person's life coexist with the present because they continually recur in memory. Willy Loman lives his past and present simultaneously. His two sons, Biff and Hap, are fun-loving, athletic boys and grown-up failures. Hap is a philandering retail clerk. Biff, who had looked forward to an athletic scholarship, discovered that his father had cheated on his mother, and, as Willy Loman sadly recognized, became a failure to spite his father. Linda Loman, the strongest character in the drama, speaks up for her husband: "Willy Loman never made a lot of money. His name was never in the paper. He's not the finest character that ever lived. But he's a human being, and a terrible thing is happening to him. So attention must be paid. He's not to be allowed to fall into his grave like an old dog."[8]

Death of a Salesman and other Miller plays, especially *A View from a Bridge* (1955), exemplify principles Miller articulates in his renowned essay "Tragedy and the Common Man." According to Aristotle's *Poetics*, the tragic hero must be an individual of high stature. To the contrary, Miller insists, "the commonest of men may take on that stature to the extent of his willingness to throw all he has into the contest, the battle to secure his rightful place in his world." The story of any "character who is ready to lay down his life, if need be, to secure one thing—his sense of personal dignity" can make exceptional tragedy.[9]

Miller's view is not unprecedented. It extends a democratic impulse that forms a pivotal aspect of American culture. Nearly a hundred years earlier Herman Melville had said much the same thing in *Moby-Dick*, as Ishmael explains how he will ascribe to the "meanest mariners, and renegades and castaways . . . high qualities" and "weave round them tragic graces."[10] Similarly, Miller weaves tragic grandeur around Willy Loman, the tragic grandeur that any man who stands up for himself deserves. *Death of a Salesman* continues to be produced, and the ideas it represents have engrained themselves in the national psyche. The phrase "like Willie Loman" has become a proverbial comparison, and Willie Loman, a tragic everyman, has become an icon of American culture.

TENNESSEE WILLIAMS

While establishing his reputation as a playwright in the late 1930s, Thomas Lanier Williams decided to change his name. His decision to call himself Tennessee Williams seems motivated by impulses that are contradictory, yet typically American. Williams wanted to establish an identity all his own, yet he also wanted to honor his family heritage. He was born in Mississippi, but his father's roots were in Tennessee. While denying his Christian name, his new name pays tribute to both his father and his southern roots. Like that of fellow Mississippian William Faulkner, much of Tennessee Williams's work explores what it means to be a southerner.

Williams's writings honor his national literary heritage as well. In *The Glass Menagerie* (1945) Amanda Wingfield refers to Benjamin Franklin. In *A Streetcar Named Desire* (1947) Blanche DuBois, shocked by the appearance of Stella's seedy New Orleans apartment, makes a literary comparison: "Never, never, never in my worst dreams could

Figure 6.2 James Kavallines, *Andy Warhol and Tennessee Williams Talking on the S.S. France.* Photographic print, 1967. Library of Congress, Prints and Photographs Division (reproduction number LC-USZ62-121294).

I picture—Only Poe! Only Mr. Edgar Allan Poe!—could do it justice! Out there I suppose is the ghoul-haunted woodland of Weir!"[11] Blanche's reference to the eerie imagery of "Ulalume" indicates her background as an English teacher and links her character to the Gothic and Romantic traditions. And *The Night of the Iguana* (1961) takes its epigraph from Emily Dickinson's "I Died for Beauty—But Was Scarce," a poem foreshadowing action late in the play.

Of all Williams's dramas, perhaps none embodies ideas central to American literature more fully than *The Night of the Iguana*. Two of its principal characters, Lawrence Shannon and Hannah Jelkes, can trace their roots to colonial America. Now defrocked and working as a tour guide, the Rev. Dr. Shannon is a direct descendant of two colonial Virginia governors and thus represents the South. Jelkes travels with her ninety-seven-year-old grandfather. Familiarly known as Nonno, her grandfather is a poet named Jonathan Coffin. Williams thus aligns him with the long-standing New England stereotype of Yankee Jonathan. His last name also has New England associations. "Coffin" is a common name in Nantucket, according to Ishmael in *Moby-Dick*, who understandably finds the name ominous. Jelkes herself represents two characteristic types, the New England spinster and the Yankee trader. She supports their travels by working as a quick-sketch artist, drawing and selling caricatures of tourists.

The drama takes place at a Mexican hotel in Puerto Vallarta run by Maxine Faulk. During the story, two local men catch an iguana and tie it up with a length of rope so that it cannot escape. Shannon shares a similar plight. The length of his rope is the width of the North American continent, and he has reached the end of it. Shannon's plight differs considerably from earlier, more optimistic portrayals of the continent. Walt Whitman's "A Passage to India" (1871) pays tribute to the completion of the transcontinental railroad. Whitman saw this continental crossing as an opportunity to link

North America with India both physically and spiritually, to unite the entire world. When Shannon speaks of the "long swim to China," he is talking not about a passage to the Orient but about a way out of the world, a way to end his seemingly farcical life.

Williams establishes traditional North/South distinctions between Miss Jelkes and the Rev. Dr. Shannon only to reconcile them the night the drama takes place, a night when she helps him through a dark and troublesome time as they talk between rooms like Emily Dickinson's two kinsmen. Though Shannon is attracted to Jelkes, she is set in her ways and has no intention of staying with him once she sees him through this one difficult night. Maxine, who also finds Shannon attractive, resents Jelkes's presence and jealously watches the two become close.

Unlike both Hannah and Shannon, Maxine has virtually no past. She was married until her husband's recent death, but otherwise Williams reveals nothing else about her life. Her past is forgotten. She lives for the present and wants Shannon to join her in it. Having failed as a tour guide, he imagines writing his bishop and returning to the Episcopal Church: that is his pipe dream. At the play's end, Faulk invites him down to the beach for a swim, but Shannon, still emotionally and physically fragile, expresses uncertainty about climbing the hill from the beach. "I'll get you back up the hill," Maxine reassures him. She has strength enough for both of them. Maxine has had no trouble leaving her past behind, and now she hopes to help Shannon break free from his.

WRITING FOR CINEMA AND TELEVISION

As an undergraduate, Sam Peckinpah directed *The Glass Menagerie*, *A Streetcar Named Desire*, and some of Tennessee Williams's one-act plays as well. He adapted *The Glass Menagerie* as a one-hour drama. Many years later he observed, "I think I learned more about writing from having to cut *Menagerie* than anything I've done since."[12] For his master's thesis, Peckinpah directed Williams's *Portrait of a Madonna* for the stage, redirected it for television, and compared the result. He chose this play partly because he found it representative of its author's work: "The theme of the play, as in most of Mr. Williams's work, lies in the ability of his characters—defeated and broken by society and their own inadequacies—to meet their fate with courage and dignity."[13] Peckinpah later called Tennessee Williams "America's greatest playwright."[14]

The close ties between Williams and Peckinpah indicate the close ties between writing for the stage and writing for cinema and television. Historians of dramatic literature have hesitated to broach this link, but it deserves consideration. The best writing ever done for television and cinema rivals writing for the stage. The problem is that the complex production process for motion pictures sometimes obscures the clarity of the author's original vision. Edward Albee, who has written some of the most challenging and innovative stage plays of the last half century—*Who's Afraid of Virginia Woolf?* (1962), *Three Tall Women* (1991)—dislikes the idea of writing for the cinema. He observed, "If you're a playwright, you control what happens to your work. If you write for movies, you don't even own the copyright on what you write, and your work can be changed without your permission."[15]

Peckinpah himself thrived as an author and director when producers gave him creative control. He did some excellent writing for several different television series—*Gunsmoke, The Rifleman, The Westerner, Zane Grey Theater*—but he had more difficulty when he turned to feature film production, when more money was involved and overzealous producers sought to protect their investments.

Perhaps no other writer in the history of cinema and television has achieved more artistic control over his material than

Paddy Chayefsky. He established his reputation while writing for *Philco Television Playhouse* (1948–55), a distinguished anthology drama series that broadcast live performances of literary adaptations and original teleplays. Gore Vidal, who is now best known as a novelist, also began his career writing teleplays for *Philco Television Playhouse*.

Marty, Chayefsky's most renowned *Philco* script, aired on May 24, 1953. *Marty* tells an emotional story of a lonely Bronx butcher who blossoms late and finds love. It, too, belongs to the drama of the everyday, plays such as those of O'Neill, Miller, and Williams that give the common man a sense of grandeur. When television production shifted from New York to Hollywood in the late 1950s, Chayefsky, a native New Yorker, stayed home and wrote for the theater, but his stage plays never achieved the critical acclaim his teleplays had.

Chayefsky returned to form when he turned to the cinema. *The Americanization of Emily* (1964) is set in England in the time before D-Day and stars James Garner as Lt. Cmdr. Charles E. Madison, a type of army officer known as a dog robber, someone whose job it is to procure whatever luxury items are essential for keeping generals happy and thus for keeping the war running smoothly. The speeches Chayefsky wrote for Garner are stirring. Both *The Hospital* (1971) and *Network* (1976) combine provocative writing with dark humor to form comments on the twisted state of society in the 1970s, but also to demonstrate, as Arthur Miller might say, man's capacity to stand up for his own personal dignity. In Chayefsky's famous words, as performed by Peter Finch in *Network*: "I'm mad as hell, and I'm not going to take it anymore."

The Hospital reveals Chayefsky's style and outlook. As it begins, Dr. Herbert Bock borders on the verge of suicide. Work is all he needs, he tells his boss, expressing an individualistic, characteristically American solution to mental illness. Having failed as a husband and a father, he takes pride in his career, defining himself through his work, but even that comes under question when a man named Drummond, formerly a physician and currently working with his daughter Barbara as a missionary among the Apaches in Mexico, arrives for a physical but nearly dies at the hands of the hospital.

Barbara Drummond approaches Dr. Bock, and in a brilliantly paced scene the two exchange long and poignant speeches as they explain their problems to each other. Bock delivers a sardonic paean to impotence, making the slogans of the contemporary counterculture his own: "Impotence is beautiful, baby! Power to the Impotent! Right on, baby!" In a calmer mood, he elaborates, "When I say I'm impotent, I mean I've lost even my desire for work, which is a hell of a lot more primal a passion than sex." He cuts their conversation short so he can get back to committing suicide. She saves him and submits to his awkward attempts to make love.

As their relationship develops, a series of murders occurs in the hospital. Having awakened from his coma, Drummond has had a vision prompting him to kill his caregivers. He does not murder anyone directly but causes their deaths by subjecting them to the hospital's care. Nurse Campanella, he decides, would "die of the great American plague—vestigial identity." This disturbing phrase expresses the idea that our identities are no longer within us but solely recorded in the equipage of modern existence. The man who loses his identification card loses his identity. Drummond sedates Nurse Campanella and straps onto her the identity bracelet of a patient scheduled for a hysterectomy. No one, not even the surgeon, notices the switch. She dies on the operating table essentially because she is wearing someone else's identity.

Earlier, Barbara had invited Bock to Mexico, but he refused: "I suppose if I'm married to anything, it's this hospital. It's been my whole life. I just can't walk out on it as if it never mattered. I'm middle-class. Among us middle-class, love doesn't triumph over all. Responsibility does." In light of the bizarre developments, he agrees to accompany her, but as the drama ends, he once more refuses, telling her, "The hospital's coming apart. I can't walk out on it when it's coming apart. Somebody has to be responsible, Barbara. Everybody's hitting the road, running to the hills, running away. Somebody's got to be responsible." *The Hospital* elevates the acceptance of responsibility to a heroic act.

In the late 1970s, Paddy Chayefsky called *The Rockford Files* (1974–80) his favorite television series.[16] His appreciation testifies to the fine writing that went into the series, which pays homage to Chayefsky's work. Jim Rockford, the character James Garner plays in the series, is an extension of Charles Madison, the character he had played in *The Americanization of Emily*. Rockford had been a dog robber in the Korean War, and he applies his wartime skills in his role as a private investigator. Creator Roy Huggins, who wrote pulp fiction before turning to television, devised many of the plots for the first season of the show. Stephen J. Cannell, who has been compared to British playwright Tom Stoppard, wrote several episodes.[17] And Juanita Bartlett wrote some of the most memorable episodes of the series.

Guest writers added further élan. For "The Four Pound Brick," an episode from the first season, Leigh Brackett came up with the story and co-wrote the teleplay with Bartlett. Considered the finest female author in the typically testosterone-laden genre of hard-boiled detective fiction, Brackett also wrote for the cinema. With William Faulkner, she adapted Raymond Chandler's novel as *The Big Sleep* (1946). She also wrote the screenplay for *Hatari!* (1962). And she co-wrote *The Empire Strikes Back* (1980) with Lawrence Kasdan.

"The Four Pound Brick," a story of police corruption inspired by Sidney Lumet's *Serpico* (1973), contains many memorable lines. The episode begins at a funeral, where Kate Banning is burying her son, a young policeman who has died in the line of duty. She complains that the cemetery would not allow her to put up a headstone, just a "brass plaque flush to the ground so it don't get in the way of the lawnmower." Her realistically flawed grammar reveals her lack of education, but she has an intuitive insight that no amount of education can provide. Disliking the cemetery's neatness, she comments, "I think graves ought to be a little untidy, the way lives are."

One problem with trying to write the literary history of television is that television writing in recent years typically has been done by committee. Some of the most creative writing in the United States today is being done by the staff writers for *The Simpsons* (1989–), the credits of which often list multiple writers for each episode. After an episode airs, the witty sayings their authors carefully crafted are attributed to whichever character on the show that says them; the authors are forgotten. The challenge of writing for television nowadays is a matter of finding ways to impose individual personality onto a group project.

Unlike so many other television writers, Larry David and Jerry Seinfeld have successfully created work that embodies their individuality. As co-creators of *Seinfeld* (1991–99), they have been responsible for some of the smartest writing television has seen in recent decades. *Seinfeld* often looks to the history of American literature for inspiration, freely raiding well-respected dramatic literature. In "The Pen" (1991), an episode written by Larry David, Elaine (Julia Louis-Dreyfus) shows up at a retirees' party whacked out on muscle relaxants, meets a woman named Stella, and proceeds to yell "Stella!" in the manner of Stanley Kowalski in *A Streetcar Named Desire*. In "The Subway" (1992), George Costanza

(Jason Alexander)—the character Larry David based on himself—boards the subway for a job interview. Beforehand, Jerry warns him not to whistle on the elevator. When George asks why not, Jerry reminds him that Willy Loman gave his son Biff similar advice in *Death of a Salesman*. George is shocked that Jerry would compare him to Biff Loman, whom George calls "the biggest loser in the history of American literature."

With its allusions to the work of Tennessee Williams and Arthur Miller, *Seinfeld* does what Williams himself did when he alluded to Emily Dickinson, Benjamin Franklin, and Edgar Allan Poe: pay homage to literary progenitors. American literature forms a shared language and a shared heritage. Allusions provide a shorthand for the complex concepts the literature embodies. Like so many of the major stage plays in American literature, *Seinfeld*, too, is a drama of the everyday. That it can allude to literary characters, themes, and plots as it treats such mundane tasks as finding a parking space, ordering soup at a deli, or waiting for a table at a restaurant indicates how integral American literature is to the everyday.

Chapter 7

The Great American Novel

THE BIRTH OF A LITERARY IDEAL

"The dream of the great American novel is past." So wrote Maxine Hong Kingston at the end of the 1980s. Her words sound absolute, but in light of her own literary career, her statement takes on a curious ambiguity. It occurs in an essay she wrote after *Tripmaster Monkey*, which she had deliberately fashioned as the great American novel.[1] Was Kingston saying the dream was over because she had accomplished the task? Or was she speaking more generally, asserting that this long-standing literary ideal was losing its validity as the twenty-first century approached? To start answering these questions, let's go back to 1867, the year this famous phrase was coined.

When the copywriters at Sheldon and Company, a New York publisher, were searching for ways to promote Rebecca Harding Davis's *Waiting for the Verdict* (1867), they came up with "The Great American Novel." The first published advertisement for this novel represents the phrase's earliest known usage. By the time this book appeared, Davis had established her reputation with "Life in the Iron Mills" (1861), a short story that is considered a pioneering work of American literary realism, telling a tale of poverty and privation. *Waiting for the Verdict*, which Davis wrote as a kind of Reconstructionist *Uncle Tom's Cabin*, perpetuated her interest in the plight of the downtrodden. Reviewing the novel, Henry James called Davis "the poet of the poor people."[2] Though she did not start with the intention of writing the great American novel, the book partly justifies the advertising copy in terms of its broad geographic scope and its willingness to broach major issues facing the United States after the Civil War.

Waiting for the Verdict intertwines two love stories: one about Rosslyn Burley, a Northern abolitionist of illegitimate birth, and Garrick Randolph, an aristocratic southerner and slaveholder, and the second about Margaret Conrad, a small-minded preacher's daughter, and Dr. John Broderip, a biracial surgeon who passes as white. The first couple reconciles their regional, political, and social differences and marries happily. When Broderip reveals his secret to his supposedly altruistic lover, she rejects him and, in so doing, reveals her hypocrisy. *Waiting for the Verdict* contains some moving passages, but the novel is hindered by improbable coincidence, overt Christian moralizing, and flawed character development.

Though *Waiting for the Verdict*, aesthetically speaking, was not the major novel it claimed to be, its advertising copy had a lasting impact on critical discourse. The appeal of the copywriters' phrase is easy to understand. The desire for a literary work commensurate with the greatness of the United States stretches back to late eighteenth-century efforts to create a national epic poem. During the final third of the nineteenth century, the novel was emerging as the foremost genre of American literature. The great American novel, as it was starting to be defined, would be a national epic in prose. Within the covers of a single volume, it would encapsulate the nation.

Having started his literary career as a historian and travel writer, John De Forest later turned novelist and literary critic. He used the publication of *Waiting for the Verdict* to ponder what novels meant to the United States. In his review of the book, he suggested that the great American novel should not only have "national breadth" but also demonstrate "truthful outlining of characters, natural speaking, and plenty of strong feeling."[3] De Forest considered whether the phrase suited any extant novels. From a modern perspective, *Moby-Dick* seems the likeliest candidate among books published before *Waiting for the Verdict*, but Melville's whaling opus was much too daring to achieve widespread acceptance among nineteenth-century readers; De Forest made no mention of it. *The Scarlet Letter* (1850) remained the most well-respected work of fiction in American literature, but De Forest refused it status as the great American novel. According to him, Harriet Beecher Stowe's *Uncle Tom's Cabin* came closest to the ideal, but he concluded that the great American novel had yet to be written. Though De Forest's essay is vague about the specific requirements for this ideal novel, his comments reflect the same realist aesthetic as his own novels.

Years later Davis herself indicated what the great American novel should involve. She said that it should encompass "all the phases of our national life" and the diversity of the American people. It should include New Yorker and Navajo, Virginia gentleman and Maine leper, Jew and Catholic, African American and Italian immigrant, Molly Maguire and millionaire. Despite these suggestions, Davis was not upholding the great American novel as any kind of ideal. She called it "that much longed-for monstrosity."[4]

In 1891, the same year Davis made these remarks, James Lane Allen, a Kentucky novelist, wrote the fullest critical treatment of the idea to that time.[5] He, too, said that the great American novel had yet to be written. Allen proceeded to consider how several different novels compared to the ideal. The requirement that the great American novel take "for its material the subject of American life" disqualified some fine contemporary works. Allen excluded *The Tragic Muse* (1890), Henry James's story of Lady Agnes Dormer and the lives and loves of her talented yet fickle children, because it had a European setting and British characters.

Even novels with American characters and settings did not necessarily qualify. The great American novel could not be based on local or sectional ideas: it had to concern the nation as a whole. Like De Forest, Allen weighed earlier works as candidates. *Adventures of Huckleberry Finn* remained too controversial for consideration. *The Scarlet Letter*—the straw man of the critical discourse—could not be the great American novel in Allen's view because its Puritanism had never been a national idea.

Novels incorporating national ideas were often insufficient because their settings made them local. Helen Hunt Jackson's *Ramona* (1884), which poignantly dramatizes the conflict between land-hungry settlers and Native Americans, rests on "a truly

Figure 7.1 Joseph Ferdinand Keppler, *Mark Twain: America's Best Humourist.* Lithograph, from *Puck* 18 (16 December 1885): 256.

national idea," but the work, in Allen's view, cannot be national because its California setting localized the story. Allen's attitude reflects the contemporary reception of *Ramona*. Though written to expose the injustice of the confiscation of tribal lands by the federal government, the novel was read superficially as a romantic tale set in the idyllic land of southern California. Devoted to local color writing himself, Allen ignored the possibility of a novel with multiple settings stretching across the nation.

Though he almost denies the possibility of the great American novel altogether, Allen suggests that if the United States should go to war against a foreign power, then novelists could depict the nation unified in its struggle. On further consideration, Allen asserts that an international novel could qualify—provided it featured a representative American. In James's *Daisy Miller* (1878), the title character possesses personal traits that reflect the national character. Her innocence and her audacity prove to be a dangerous combination that charms some Europeans, offends others, and eventually leads to her demise. Allen could have used other James novels such as *Roderick Hudson* or *The Portrait of a Lady* to make his point.

James would continue to place Americans on an international stage to see how they fared. *The Ambassadors* (1903), one of the three great novels he wrote toward the end of his career (the others being *The Wings of the Dove* [1902] and *The Golden Bowl* [1904]), tells the story of Lambert Strether, a middle-aged American sent to Paris by his fiancée, Mrs. Newsome, to bring home her son Chad. While there, Strether enjoys the charm of the Old World, and Mrs. Newsome must then dispatch a cadre of ambassadors to try to bring home both Chad and Lambert. Written in a complex narrative style, *The Ambassadors* rewards patient readers with tenderhearted humor, incisive character studies, and a vivid picture of expatriate society at the turn of the century.

Figure 7.2 Bain News Service, *Henry James*. Photographic print, 30 March 1910. Library of Congress, Prints and Photographs Division, George Grantham Bain Collection (reproduction number LC-DIG-ggbain-04703).

Five years after Allen's essay, William Morton Payne similarly attempted to define the great American novel. *The Scarlet Letter* remained much too narrow in scope to qualify. The nation's ideal novel must be broad and deep. Shrewdly, Payne recognized that a work's popularity did not necessarily indicate its literary quality. Originality was an essential part of any great work, but contemporary readers typically meet original works with resistance and even belligerence. The great American novel should be "imbued with the passion of democracy," reflect "what is best and deepest in American life," "strike deep root in the soil that the centuries have prepared for our civilization," yet "be a concrete and vital presentation of certain individual lives as they are lived, or conceivably might be lived, at the present day."[6]

Almost thirty years after De Forest's article, realism remained the predominant approach to fiction, and Payne's recommendations embody this realist aesthetic. The great American novel, he continued, should be "an epic of individualism." His words stress the long-standing association between the epic and the novel and reinforce the theme of individual identity.

NEW DIRECTIONS

In his essay "The Great American Novelist" (1902), Frank Norris offered a different perspective. Whereas Allen had disqualified local novels, Norris suggested that a novel could transcend its local setting and apply to people throughout the nation. If George Washington Cable ventured "*deep enough* into the hearts and lives of his creoles, he would at last strike the universal substratum and find the elemental thing that is common to the creole and Puritan alike." Getting hold of that elemental thing, the novelist "could produce the Great American Novel that should be a picture of the entire nation."[7]

Of course, if writers delved so deeply into the national psyche to find a subject applicable to all Americans, the subject likely would apply also to readers beyond the borders. The great American novelist "would have sounded the world-note; he would be a writer not national, but international, and his countrymen would be all humanity, not the citizens of any one nation. He himself would be a heritage of the whole world." Norris concludes whimsically, asserting that "the Great American Novel is not extinct like the Dodo, but mythical like the Hippogriff."[8]

Norris's own fiction, while manifesting an epic dimension, implies that the nation cannot be circumscribed within a single volume. He conceived a three-novel trilogy, "The Epic of the

Wheat," which would treat its subject in an increasingly expansive manner: local, national, global. *The Octopus* (1901), the first work in the trilogy, depicts the clash between California wheat farmers and railroad tycoons seeking to control the land. *The Pit* (1903), which appeared the year after Norris's death, tells the story of wheat trading and speculation in the pits of the Chicago mercantile exchange. *The Wolf*, the proposed third volume in the trilogy, would have traced the fate of American wheat on the world marketplace. To tell the story of the United States, Norris's work implies, the novelist required multiple volumes set at different stages along the chain of the capitalist market system. *U.S.A.* (1938), John Dos Passos's stylistically innovative trilogy, unifies earlier novels—*The 42nd Parallel* (1930), *1919* (1932), and *The Big Money* (1936)—and also implies that it takes three to tell the national story.

In 1918 a contributor to the New York *Globe* recalled, "A favorite occupation of the American used to be to make guesses as to when, where, and how the Great American Novel would be born."[9] The comment implies that this literary quest, though unfulfilled, was a thing of the past. A new generation of American authors renewed the quest after World War I, however. To create a novel encapsulating the nation formed a goal of many young twentieth-century writers.

Working as a reporter for the *Baltimore Sun* in the early 1920s, James M. Cain visited the coal mines of West Virginia to report a sensational trial. The experience gave him an idea for a large, sweeping novel. Cain took a leave of absence from the *Sun*, hoping to produce the great American novel. After starting and abandoning three different manuscripts, he despondently admitted that his hope was unrealistic—beyond his abilities. Attempting to turn the lives of West Virginia coal miners into fiction, Cain was laboring under an old-fashioned concept of literature. His idea sounds like a subject for a naturalistic novel; the setting, in fact, is straight out of Emile Zola's *Germinal* (1885). More recently, Upton Sinclair had published *King Coal* (1917), another muckraking coal miner novel, with uneven results. Tastes had changed considerably since the Great War: naturalism had given way to modernism. Cain did not write his first novel until he abandoned naturalism and assumed a lean, tough narrative voice suitable to the times: the hard-boiled style.

The Postman Always Rings Twice (1934) possesses many elements aligning it with earlier strains in the American literary tradition. Narrator-protagonist Frank Chambers resembles Poe's first-person narrators or O'Neill's iceman, men guilty of immoral criminal acts who calmly relate their nefarious personal histories. Before coming to the Twin Oaks Tavern and getting mixed up with Nick and Cora Papadakis, Frank was a tramp. Frank's restlessness, not unlike the hobo's life Jack London portrays in *The Road* (1907), is quintessentially American, and the places he has traveled—Illinois, Kansas, South Dakota—allow him to represent the nation.

Nick also symbolizes the American dream. A Greek immigrant, he has ventured west to California, worked hard, and established a successful business. The sign for Nick's roadhouse incorporates both Greek and American flags. Cora accepts the idea of the American dream but reaches it a little late. She wants to work hard and succeed, but only after she and Frank have murdered Nick. Like so many subsequent crime novels in the hard-boiled style—Horace McCoy's *They Shoot Horses, Don't They?* (1935), a tragic tale of a marathon dance narrated in a deadpan manner; Raymond Chandler's *Farewell, My Lovely* (1940), an intricate yet fast-paced detective story depicting the interplay of the ambitious racketeers and crooked cops who people the streets of urban America; Cornell Woolrich's *I Married a Dead Man* (1948), a bleak, powerful story about the impossibility of love in a world of evil—*The Postman Always Rings Twice* is the great American novel turned inside out.

In 1923 William Carlos Williams published a book audaciously titled *The Great American Novel*. After establishing his literary career as a poet, Williams shifted to prose in the 1920s to explore his relationship with American life and culture, an interest pervading his subsequent work from *In the American Grain* (1925), a series of reflections on prominent figures in American history, through his return to verse and his triumphant American epic, *Paterson*.

The Great American Novel marks a new departure from previous attempts at definition. Gone are the character development, epic scope, and realistic detail that had been associated with the novel since the 1860s. What matters instead is not form but texture, as Ezra Pound remarked.[10] Williams himself called *The Great American Novel* "a satire on the novel form."[11] He applied James Joyce's discursive method to challenge long-standing ideas regarding the novel, America, and the idea of literary greatness.

Writing in the 1920s, Edith Wharton also challenged the idea of the great American novel. She had established her own literary reputation with three novels: *The House of Mirth* (1905), the story of Lily Bart's tragic failure to find a husband within New York's high society; *Ethan Frome* (1911), a somber tale of a man trapped in a loveless marriage who disastrously falls for his wife's charming relative; and *The Age of Innocence* (1920), a finely wrought etching of New York society in the 1870s that depicts Newland Archer, a man caught between a fiancée from conventional society and an exotic soul mate from Europe.

Wharton challenged the whole idea of a great national novel by affixing the label to Anita Loos's *Gentlemen Prefer Blondes* (1925). Another first-person narrative, *Gentlemen Prefer Blondes* is told in the form of a diary by Lorelei Lee, Loos's vivacious protagonist. Though *Gentlemen Prefer Blondes* may seem too slight a work to qualify for the prized description, Wharton's appreciation of it is understandable. Playing the dizzy blonde on the surface, Lorelei is a shrewd woman who successfully negotiates her way through American and European society to obtain whatever she wants from life. The diary format privileges her voice, giving Lorelei the first and last word regarding how gentlemen think and what they prefer: qualities she understands so well that she can manipulate them with ease.

In her essay "The Great American Novel" Wharton addresses the topic at length. She seems motivated by anger stemming from the ongoing popularity of Sinclair Lewis's *Main Street* (1920). Set in Gopher Prairie, Minnesota, *Main Street* is a send-up of small-town, midwestern America. Despite Lewis's satirical edge, his portrayal strongly influenced stereotypes about the United States around the world and, to Wharton's chagrin, reinforced the notion that the American novel should be set in a small town, that it "must always be about Main Street, geographically, socially, and intellectually."[12]

Instead, Wharton suggested the great American novel could be set anywhere in the world, using some prominent American authors to show what she meant:

> In those steamless and wireless days Poe was letting his fiery fancy range over all heaven and earth, Melville was situating his tales in the tropics, and Hawthorne coloring his with the prismatic hues of a largely imaginary historic past. Our early novelists were, in fact, instinctively choosing those scenes and situations which offered the freest range to their invention, without fear of being repudiated as un-American if they wandered beyond the twelve-mile limit.[13]

Stories of expatriates, Wharton suggested, were especially fitting topics for American novels because the expat "is peculiarly typical of modern America—of its intense social acquisitiveness and insatiable appetite for new facts and new sights."[14] Though she did not provide any examples to support this point, she may have had in mind the works of her friend Henry James. Alternatively, she may have been thinking of more recent works, such as Ernest Hemingway's expatriate novel *The Sun Also Rises* (1926), the work that defined the "Lost Generation."

Perhaps no twentieth-century work has been called the great American novel more often than *The Great Gatsby* (1925), in which F. Scott Fitzgerald poignantly synthesizes the ambitions, dreams, and delusions that defined America after World War I. Though set in the New York metropolis, the story of Jay Gatsby, according to narrator Nick Carraway, is "a story of the West." Coming from the Midwest, Nick says, all the principal characters possess "some deficiency in common which made us subtly unadaptable to Eastern life."[15] And Nick is writing from the Midwest, which shapes the story's telling. *The Great Gatsby* reinforces the importance of place in the creation of American literature, doing so in an understated yet appealing new manner.

The Great Gatsby recapitulates the concept of the American dream. As a boy, Nick tells us, Gatsby had followed a program of self-improvement patterned on the tenets of Benjamin Franklin. Gatsby ran away from his parents—"shiftless and unsuccessful farm people"—and "invented just the sort of Jay Gatsby that a seventeen-year-old boy would be likely to invent." He "sprang from his Platonic conception of himself."[16] Though Gatsby seems to exemplify the self-made man, Meyer Wolfsheim, the shady gangster who brought Gatsby into the underworld, challenges the idea. "I made him," Wolfsheim tells Nick. *The Great Gatsby* paradoxically validates yet challenges the personal motivation and self-discipline crucial to the American dream.

William Faulkner's career took a much different shape. None of the other novels Fitzgerald completed—*This Side of Paradise*

(1920), *The Beautiful and the Damned* (1922), *Tender Is the Night* (1934)—approach *The Great Gatsby* in terms of literary quality. In William Faulkner's case, no individual novel stands out. He is best known for his oeuvre—the series of novels that forms the Yoknapatawpha cycle. Unified by their setting, a fictional county located in northern Mississippi, these novels feature many enduring characters and themes.

Faulkner's trademark is the use of multiple viewpoints. *The Sound and the Fury* (1929), possibly the most challenging work in the cycle, relates the story of the Compsons, a family that has roots in the southern aristocracy but has since fallen into decay. The novel is narrated from four different points of view. Each of the three sons of Jason Compson III—Benjy, Quentin, and

Figure 7.3 Carl Van Vechten, *William Faulkner*. Photographic print, gelatin silver, 11 December 1954. Library of Congress, Prints and Photographs Division, Carl Van Vechten Collection (reproduction number LC-DIG-ppmsca-10445 DLC).

Jason—tells the story in his own way. Finally, an objective narrator retells the story. Faulkner deliberately challenged his readers by making the first section of *The Sound and the Fury* a stream-of-consciousness narrative as it unfolds in the mind of the mentally deficient Benjy. He made readers work hard to find meaning in this novel and others. An interviewer told him that some readers could not understand his writing, even after they had read it three times, and asked what advice he had for them. With a wry smile, no doubt, Faulkner replied, "Read it four times."[17]

Not all his novels are as difficult as *The Sound and the Fury*. *As I Lay Dying* (1930) tells the story of the Bundren family as they take the decomposing body of their matriarch, Addie Bundren, to be buried in the county seat. Also told from the point of view of several different characters, including the dead woman, *As I Lay Dying* is more approachable than *The Sound and the Fury*. It makes a good place for readers new to Faulkner to start.

The Hamlet (1931), the first work in the Snopes trilogy (the others being *The Town* [1957] and *The Mansion* [1959]), begins the Snopes family saga by relating the story of Flem Snopes, whose life presents an ironic perspective on the American promise of success and personal satisfaction. From a clerk at a general store, Flem rises to a position of financial power, but he does so not by hard work and determination but by double-dealing and connivery.

The novels in Faulkner's Yoknapatawpha cycle reflect the life of twentieth-century rural Mississippi. But Faulkner's personal vision and daring prose let him surpass the role of local colorist. Faulkner is the author Norris looked forward to in his essay "The Great American Novelist." His novels transcend their locale to apply to the nation, nay, to mankind as a whole. They have been acclaimed throughout the world and translated into Arabic, Croatian, Hindi, Korean, Vietnamese, and dozens of other languages.

Few could argue with the proposition that William Faulkner may be the greatest American novelist of the twentieth century. Any such debate usually has Faulkner at its center.

THE POSTMODERN NOVEL

The period from the late 1950s to the mid-1960s gave rise to many groundbreaking novels. Jack Kerouac's *On the Road* (1957)—the bible of the Beat Generation—tells the story of Sal Paradise and Dean Moriarty, thinly veiled versions of the contemplative Kerouac and the hyperkinetic Neal Cassady, as they crisscross North America in search of art, friendship, life, love, and satori. Since the *History of the Expedition Under the Command of Captains Lewis and Clark*, the transcontinental journey has formed a cornerstone of American literature. In terms of cultural history, the lifestyle Kerouac depicts in both *On the Road* and his follow-up novel *The Dharma Bums* (1958) modeled a behavioral pattern for the counterculture of the sixties and early seventies. But his writing style may be more influential than his lifestyle. Inspired by jazz improvisation, Kerouac's "spontaneous prose" values accident, risk, and self-indulgence for what they can contribute to artistic expression.

Joseph Heller's *Catch-22* (1961) is the finest, and funniest, novel to result from the American experience in World War II. "I don't know if anyone would call it THE Great American Novel," Heller commented. "That assumes there can only be one. But, asked if it is *a* Great American Novel, I would have to say . . . it is *the* great novel of the decade.'"[18] A more objective account may place one or two of Ken Kesey's novels ahead of *Catch-22. One Flew over the Cuckoo's Nest* (1962) first comes to mind, but *Sometimes a Great Notion* (1964) is more ambitious and innovative.

While making use of many traditional American themes, *Sometimes a Great Notion* applies an unprecedented narrative strategy: the variable point of view. The narrative often switches from third to first person or from one first-person narrator to another, leaving readers to play catch-up to figure out who is saying what. Even when he maintains a third-person voice, Kesey occasionally switches focalization, providing details from the perspective of one character after another. He skips around in terms of chronology as well. In addition, he provides numerous self-reflexive comments on the narrative process itself, such as thanking "the miracle of modern narrative technique."[19]

Looming over this novel is a larger-than-life hero named Hank Stamper, whose forceful personality mixes belligerence, bravado, courage, determination, ingenuity, and just plain stubbornness. Shoulder to shoulder with Captain Ahab, Hank Stamper stands with the line of memorable, sharply etched characters in the history of the American novel. As the leader of an Oregon logging family, he confronts anyone and everyone who tries to wrest his business from him. He is a paragon of that attribute so often ascribed to the West: American individuality.

Though Kesey showed that American tradition and innovation could come together to produce an extraordinary novel, *Sometimes a Great Notion* could be seen as marking the end of a major literary period instead of the beginning. The year after it appeared, Donald Barthelme published *Snow White* (1965), which effectively sounded the death knell of the American novel as an evolving and coherent form. The text of Barthelme's novel, a postmodern redaction of the traditional fairy tale, offers a key to what happened to the novel. When Snow White is asked why she continues to live with the seven dwarfs, she responds, "It must be laid, I suppose, to a failure of the imagination. I have not been able to imagine anything better."[20] So, too, the American novelist of the late sixties, a time when many of the best writers turned toward nonfiction.

THE NEW JOURNALISM AND THE DEATH OF THE NOVEL

Tom Wolfe assessed what had happened during the 1960s in his essay "Why They Aren't Writing the Great American Novel Anymore." Since the novel's emergence, a literary class system had developed, one that made novelists the aristocracy and journalists the plebeians. In the 1960s, however, journalists began using novelistic techniques: taking innovative narrative approaches, making strategic use of recurring motifs, and incorporating extensive dialogue. The work of these New Journalists, as they came to be called, was not without antecedents. Lillian Ross's *Picture* (1952), which chronicled John Huston's frustrating struggle to bring Stephen Crane's *Red Badge of Courage* (1895) to the cinema, is one influential precursor. But in the sixties, New Journalists took center stage and flourished as literary voices for the age.

Though the journalists' literary techniques resembled the novelists', their work habits differed. Whereas novelists could use their imaginations to create dialogue, journalists had to endear themselves to their subjects, spending long periods of time with them and gaining their confidence to such an extent that they would agree to be tape-recorded. To write book-length, novel-like works, journalists had to immerse themselves thoroughly in the milieu of their subjects, so thoroughly that their argot and mindset would become second nature. Being a New Journalist required an open mind, dogged determination, and considerable freedom from other obligations.

Wolfe identified a continuity between the realism of the late nineteenth-century novelists and what New Journalists wanted to do, that is, get reality down on paper, something novelists such as Barthelme could no longer stomach. The novelists' rejection of reality is understandable. As a literary approach, realism was already wearing thin by the start of the twentieth century. To advance their craft, novelists had to abandon realism, but doing so required a vast leap of the imagination, which most were unable to take. Consequently, journalists, in Wolfe's characteristic words, "had the whole crazed obscene uproarious Mammon-faced drug-soaked mau-mau lust-oozing Sixties in America all to ourselves."[21]

With *The Electric Kool-Aid Acid Test* (1968), Wolfe provided some continuity between the great American novel and the "nonfiction novel," to use a phrase Truman Capote coined to characterize his famous contribution to New Journalism, *In Cold Blood* (1966). Wolfe took Ken Kesey for his subject, describing him at a moment when he had quit writing. Instead, Kesey sought new forms of creative expression, which mainly involved him and his followers—the Merry Pranksters—taking massive quantities of LSD, driving a Day-Glo bus across the continent (with none other than Neal Cassady of *On the Road* fame at the wheel), and trying to unsettle—"freak out"—the establishment. So a curious hybrid emerged. *The Electric Kool-Aid Acid Test* is a novel-like work of nonfiction about a novelist who no longer writes fiction.

THE GENRE THAT WOULDN'T DIE

As New Journalism proliferated with such works as Hunter S. Thompson's *Hell's Angels* (1967), Joan Didion's *Slouching Towards Bethlehem* (1968), Gay Talese's *Honor Thy Father* (1971), and Peter

Maas's *Serpico* (1973), novelists grew restless. Unmoved or unwilling to take the kinds of personal risks the New Journalists were taking—Talese with the Mafia, Thompson with the Hell's Angels—the novelists resented the journalists for the attention and acclaim they were receiving. They decided to revitalize their imaginations and start manipulating the written word in new and original ways. Perhaps none of the novelists of the period had a better imagination or greater word-manipulating skill than Philip Roth.

Published the year after Wolfe's "Why They Aren't Writing the Great American Novel Anymore," Roth's *The Great American Novel* (1973) essentially offers a four-hundred-page refutation to Wolfe's essay. Early on, Roth situates the book within the history of American literature. For his epigraph, he quotes Frank Norris's comparison between the great American novel and the mythical hippogriff. Roth's lengthy prologue recalls "The Custom-House," Hawthorne's introduction to *The Scarlet Letter*. In his prologue—an absolute tour de force—Roth's narrator, a sports journalist by the name of Smith, first name Word, does things with words no real-life journalist would dare to do.

Late in the prologue, after an imaginary conversation between Ernest Hemingway and a Vassar student, Word Smith identifies his precursors in the competition for the great American novel: *The Scarlet Letter*, *Moby-Dick*, and *Huckleberry Finn*. The remainder of Roth's novel cannot match the virtuosity of its prologue or meet the promise of its ambitious title, but it is the greatest baseball novel ever written, besting the previous titleholder, Bernard Malamud's *The Natural* (1961).

Tom Wolfe continued to exemplify New Journalism with his grand saga of space travel, *The Right Stuff* (1979). At the time of its publication, Wolfe ranked among the best authors in America—despite his often annoying idiosyncrasies. ("He uses more exclamation points than any American author," Lisa Simpson quips.) Still, a nagging critique persisted: if Wolfe was such a good writer, people asked, then why hadn't he written a novel? As much as he had tried to elevate the role of journalist to that of great writer, Wolfe still had not toppled the established literary hierarchy that keeps novelists on top. He eventually silenced his critics with a series of ambitious if uneven novels: *The Bonfire of the Vanities* (1987), *A Man in Full* (1998), and *I Am Charlotte Simmons* (2004).

Maxine Hong Kingston faced a similar situation. She established her reputation with *The Woman Warrior: Memoirs of a Girlhood Among Ghosts* (1976) and extended it with *China Men* (1980). Both books are challenging combinations of history, legend, memoir, and short story, but some readers felt that she still had to prove herself with a novel proper. The result was *Tripmaster Monkey*, an attempt to chronicle the male Asian American experience. *Tripmaster Monkey* falls short of her earlier and more innovative works. Neither is it as good as other novels with a similar purpose, such as Younghill Kang's *East Goes West: The Making of an Oriental Yankee* (1937) or, more recently, Chang-Rae Lee's *Native Speaker* (1995). Despite its shortcomings, *Tripmaster Monkey*, like *Bonfire of the Vanities*, did silence the critics.

In place of the great American novel, Kingston proposed an alternative, a "Global novel." She observed: "The danger is that the Global novel has to imitate chaos: loaded guns, bombs, leaking boats, broken-down civilizations, a hole in the sky, broken English, people who refuse connections with others. How to stretch the novel to comprehend our times—no guarantees of inherent or eventual order—without it falling apart? How to integrate the surreal, society, our psyches?"[22] Kingston's idea for the global novel is intriguing, perhaps, but it is not exactly new. Didn't Frank Norris say much the same thing when he suggested that the great American novel would reflect thoughts and feelings with worldwide appeal?

Though Kingston tried to place the great American novel in the past, the phrase continues to be used. In the twenty-first century, perhaps it has been applied to no single novel more than to Jonathan Franzen's *The Corrections* (2001). Franzen does what Wolfe said novelists were no longer willing to do: write a story of social realism. In a simple yet elegantly structured narrative, he tells the story of the Lamberts, an upper-middle-class family with a retired husband on the verge of mental collapse, a wife whose sole desire is to reunite her family for Christmas, and three unlikable but paradoxically sympathetic adult children whose individual neuroses continually sabotage their professional success. As Lisa Simpson says about *The Corrections*, "It makes me feel better about my own family."

Franzen has continued to cultivate the image of the great American novelist, depicting himself in countless interviews as the angst-ridden writer who spends years devising plot and character. Nine years passed between *The Corrections* and Franzen's next novel, but sure enough, with the appearance of *Freedom* (2010)—another saga of a midwestern family in tatters—the term "great American novel" began to be bandied about again. The general consensus is that *Freedom* is not nearly as great, or even as good, as *The Corrections*, but the new book's inadequacies have not shaken the mantle of great American novelist from Franzen's shoulders.

The week before *Freedom* appeared, Franzen got his picture on the cover of *Time*, a distinction he shares with only a few other American novelists: Toni Morrison, J. D. Salinger, John Updike. The caption on the cover labels him "Great American Novelist." Lev Grossman's feature article provides a more balanced view. Whereas so many recent novels are narrowly focused, Grossman argues, Franzen uses a wide-angle lens: he manages to keep much in focus simultaneously.[23] Eschewing the narrative experimentation of other early twenty-first-century novelists, Franzen concentrates his attention on plot and character. The fact that Franzen is called the great American novelist more readily than his contemporaries may indicate the reactionary quality of that label. Perhaps experimentation must be sacrificed to write a novel such as *The Corrections*, that is, one that millions of readers enjoy, but a truly great novel, American or not, requires more daring. To write the great American novel an author faces a double challenge. The author must not only tell a story that encapsulates the nation but also tell it in a new way, inventing a mode and method of storytelling different from what other novelists have done before. Novelists with the ambition, talent, and daring to accept this challenge come along only once or twice a century.

Chapter 8

Endings

Naming the hero of *The American* (1877) Christopher Newman, Henry James let him embody a defining trait of the American national character: the individual's capacity to remake himself or herself into a new person, to shrug off an old identity and take on a new one. The name exemplifies Crèvecoeur's definition of "the American": "a new man, who acts upon new principles."[1] But this realist novel is not filled with jingoistic platitudes. In it Henry James takes an unsentimental, steely-eyed look at what it means to be an American. Lifting Newman from a comfortable home in the land where he made his fortune, James transplants him to Europe to see how he fares outside his element.

Newman's life in the United States constituted a familiar version of the success story. He worked hard, got ahead, and struck it rich, all while a young man. As *The American* begins, Newman has traveled to Europe to acquire the personal trappings that have so far eluded him, hoping that some of the charm and cultural sophistication of the Old World will rub off on him. In Paris he meets Mme. Claire de Cintré, a widow of noble birth whom he courts. She hesitantly accepts his marriage proposal, but faced with her aristocratic family's ongoing disapproval of a man who made his money in manufacturing, she breaks their engagement and enters a convent to become a nun. After he comes into possession of a scandalous family secret, Newman considers using it to get his way with her but decides against doing so.

In the final chapter, he places a scrap of paper that holds the family secret into the fire. The novel closes with a melancholy image of loss: "Newman instinctively turned to see if the little paper was in fact consumed; but there was nothing left of it."[2] Some contemporary American readers were dissatisfied with this conclusion. The reviewer for the *New York Times* suggested that James should have "blown the convent up with nitroglycerine, and had Newman carry off Mme. de Cintré on an engine captured and managed for that purpose by the hero himself, than to have allowed him to end his love affair in what is vulgarly termed a fizzle."[3] This alternative—a blend of sentiment and derring-do—indicates that what is known as the Hollywood ending long predated the invention of motion pictures. The popular fiction of James's day was filled with stories ending with hero and heroine reunited after a series of action-packed adventures. But in *The American*, as in many of his subsequent novels, James avoided conventional endings. Instead, he often closed his novels with ambiguity and uncertainty.

As a representative American, Newman in the end faces a dilemma. His background as a go-getting, self-made man should prompt him to take action to get what he wants. But the only way to accomplish that end is to make use of the past—Mme. de Cintré's family secret—a means that conflicts with the typically American impulse to forget the past. To follow one impulse, Newman must deny the other. He chooses to forget the past. Traditionally, emigrants from the Old World came to the New to remake themselves. Paradoxically, Christopher Newman visits the Old World, where he nonetheless remakes himself into someone different from who he was when he first came to Europe, a sadder and a wiser man, perhaps, but a new man nonetheless. He accepts the loss of Mme. de Cintré and, in so doing, accepts the loss of other characteristics that had formerly made him a representative successful American. With these losses comes something positive, a newfound integrity that prevents him from using another's dirty little secrets to get his way.

The elegiac tone of James's ending is not unusual in American literature. Opportunities for people in the United States to make themselves into whomever they wish would seem to offer much optimism, but a similar sense of loss often accompanies the portrayal of Americans in metamorphosis. Whoever assumes a new identity, after all, forgets the former self and erases the past. Many works of American literature end as this new man or new woman begins life afresh but reflects wistfully on what has been lost.

In 1844 Edgar Allan Poe wrote two tales in quick succession that depict opposite ways of reacting to the past: "The Oblong Box" and "The Premature Burial." In the first, the recently widowed Cornelius Wyatt books passage from South Carolina to New York aboard the *Independence*, bringing his wife's corpse north for a proper burial. The *Independence* wrecks at sea, but the passengers make it into the lifeboats. When the captain refuses to save the box, however, Wyatt leaves the safety of the lifeboat, returns to the *Independence*, and lashes himself to his wife's coffin, determined to save or go down with it. The coffin sinks quickly into the sea, drowning Wyatt as it goes.

Suffering from catalepsy, the narrator of "The Premature Burial" builds several safety precautions into the family vault to guard against premature burial, but apparently he falls into a cataleptic state while away from home and is buried in a distant grave. Upon waking, he shrieks for help. As it turns out, he has not been buried alive. Instead he has awoken suddenly from a sound sleep in the narrow berth of a small sloop. The experience proves therapeutic. The narrator explains: "I thought upon other subjects than Death. I discarded my medical books. 'Buchan' I burned. I read no 'Night Thoughts'—no fustian about churchyards—no bugaboo tales—*such as this*."[4]

Figure 8.1 W. S. Hartshorn and C. T. Tatman, *Edgar Allan Poe*. 1904 photograph of 1848 daguerreotype. Library of Congress, Prints and Photographs Division (reproduction number LC-USZ62-10610).

"The Oblong Box" and "The Premature Burial" can be read as companion pieces. Wyatt drowns because he refuses to let go of his dead wife's body. He symbolizes anyone and everyone brought down because they cling to the past. Whether it comes in the form of an outmoded philosophy, an outdated aesthetic, or whatever, the past can bring down anyone who holds too tightly to it. Setting aside William Buchan's *Domestic Medicine* and Edward Young's *Night Thoughts*—popular British works of the previous century—the narrator of "The Premature Burial," on the other hand, puts the past behind him, thus jettisoning his excess cultural baggage and saving himself. He explains, "In short, I became a new man, and lived a man's life. From that memorable night, I dismissed forever my charnal apprehensions, and with them vanished the cataleptic disorder, of which, perhaps, they had been less the consequence than the cause."[5]

A decade after Poe's two short stories appeared, Herman Melville treated similar ideas in "Benito Cereno," which explores the meaning of the American national character, contrasting the impulse to forget with the refusal to let go. "Benito Cereno" presents a fictional retelling of an actual shipboard slave uprising, which the real-life Captain Amasa Delano originally told in *Narrative of Voyages and Travels, in the Northern and Southern Hemispheres* (1817). Melville's story contrasts the New World with the Old, bringing together a fictionalized version of Delano, "the American," with Don Benito Cereno, "the Spaniard," whose slave ship has been taken over by its cargo, led by an African named Babo, who poses as Cereno's servant when Delano comes aboard.

The story depicts Delano as a "blunt-thinking American," one whose good nature, innocence, naïveté, and trustfulness prevent him from even recognizing the slave revolt until it glares before his eyes. Like George Wilkins Kendall in *Narrative of the Texan Santa Fé Expedition*, Delano represents the American's willingness to walk into danger without realizing the consequences. Benito Cereno, a representative of the Old World, clings to the past, a world in ruin. His ship symbolizes his attitude, its castellated forecastle resembling "some ancient turret, long ago taken by assault, and then left to decay."[6]

The real-life Delano had included several pertinent legal documents toward the end of his account, and Melville followed suit. Though Melville meticulously revised the documents, some contemporary readers disliked them, especially G. W. Curtis, the author of *The Potiphar Papers* (1853), a series of breezy satirical sketches Melville had slyly lampooned in another short story,

"Jimmy Rose" (1855). Critiquing "Benito Cereno," Curtis remarked: "It is a great pity he did not work it up as a connected tale instead of putting in the dreary documents at the end."[7] Curtis's critique of Melville's ending ignores what comes after the documents: a moving coda that brings Delano and Cereno together for a final conversation, which, incidentally, Ralph Ellison mined for an epigraph to *The Invisible Man*.

As they discuss what has happened, Delano conveys his American optimism while Cereno, visibly shaken by the slave revolt, continues to brood. Delano urges him to cheer up and even tells him how. "But the past is passed; why moralize upon it?" he says. "Forget it. See, yon bright sun has forgotten it all, and the blue sea, and the blue sky; these have turned over new leaves."

"Because they have no memory," Cereno responds dejectedly, "because they are not human."[8]

Delano lets Cereno's comment pass, but it offers a powerful counterpoint to the optimistic American philosophy he espouses. Anyone who willingly forgets the past is not fully human, Cereno essentially says. The sea, the sky: they have no memories, but man does. To deny memory is to deny an essential part of what makes us human. Delano's advice offers a coping strategy: put the past behind you, and you can start afresh. Cling to the past, and it will destroy you. The fate of Benito Cereno bears out memory's potentially destructive power. In the story's final sentence, the narrator reports that Cereno died just three months after the revolt. Happy oblivion or fatal remembrance: the situation of Amasa Delano and Benito Cereno offers no middle ground.

With *Their Eyes Were Watching God* (1937), Zora Neale Hurston found a way to reconcile loss and memory. This novel tells the story of Janie Crawford, a young woman who has been raised by her grandmother, a former slave. Given her oppressive background,

Janie's grandmother cannot imagine the possibilities that await her granddaughter. Instead, she arranges a marriage between Janie and Logan Killicks, a much older man who treats his bride scarcely better than he treats his mule. Janie leaves Logan to marry Joe Starks, who has promised to treat her right. They move to Eatonville, Florida, where Joe's leadership qualities soon make him mayor. Guided by the notion of what a mayor's wife should or should not do, Joe thinks it acceptable for Janie to work at his country store, yet unacceptable for her to loiter on the store's porch, where the town's wits and wags gather to swap stories. Dutifully, if unhappily, Janie stays with Joe until his death twenty years later. Now around forty, she soon meets a fun-loving gambler and itinerant worker nicknamed Tea Cake. Twelve years younger, Tea Cake nonetheless proves to be the love of Janie's life. He takes her to the Everglades, where they must pick beans to get by, but spend much of their time singing and dancing, eating and drinking, living and loving.

When a hurricane strikes, Tea Cake and Janie must escape the Everglades in the midst of the storm. In a tension-filled scene, a mad dog threatens Janie, but Tea Cake wrestles the dog away from her, getting bitten in the fray. Tea Cake and Janie return to the Everglades after the storm, but, having contracted rabies, he goes mad and tries to kill her. To defend herself, Janie must shoot back, killing the man she loves. With Tea Cake gone, she returns to Eatonville. Relating the experience to her friend Phoeby, Janie says, "So Ah'm back home agin and Ah'm satisfied tuh be heah. Ah done been tuh de horizon and back and now Ah kin set heah in mah house and live by comparisons."[9] As *Their Eyes Were Watching God* ends, Janie has accomplished a personal goal Hurston had set for herself in childhood. In her autobiography, *Dust Tracks on the Road*, Hurston described one of her common activities as a child: "I used to climb to the top of one of the huge Chinaberry trees which guarded our

Figure 8.2 Carl Van Vechten, *Zora Neale Hurston*. Photographic print, gelatin silver, April 3, 1938. Library of Congress, Prints and Photographs Division, Carl Van Vechten Collection (reproduction number LC-DIG-van-5a52142).

front gate, and look out over the world. The most interesting thing that I saw was the horizon. . . . It grew upon me that I ought to walk out to the horizon and see what the end of the world was like."[10]

Hurston's creative use of the horizon offers a variation on a theme that runs through American culture. In another poem that forms part of *Black Riders*, Stephen Crane had a different take on the horizon motif. The speaker of the poem sees a man pursuing the horizon. The sight disturbs him, so he accosts the man, emphasizing the futility of his pursuit. The speaker tries to tell the man that he can never catch the horizon, but before the speaker can complete what he wants to say, the running man interrupts him, calls him a liar, and hurries toward the horizon. The relation between the running man in Crane's poem and its speaker is not dissimilar to the relationship between Janie Crawford and her grandmother. One wants to chase the horizon, while the other cannot even imagine attempting such a seemingly impossible pursuit. Many other characters in American literature have chased the horizon. Janie Crawford may be the only one who catches it.

Heading to the bedroom her first night back home in Eatonville, Janie feels sad initially, but as she remembers Tea Cake, his love for her, hers for him, and all their good times together, she brightens considerably. As the book ends, we hear Janie's thoughts:

> Of course he wasn't dead. He could never be dead until she herself had finished feeling and thinking. The kiss of his memory made pictures of love and light against the wall. Here was peace. She pulled in her horizon like a great fish-net. Pulled it from around the waist of the world and draped it over her shoulder. So much of life in its meshes! She called in her soul to come and see.[11]

Not only has Janie been to the horizon, she has brought it back with her. It represents her memories, which she can reexperience whenever she wishes. She and Tea Cake were together for less than two years, but they managed to fit a lifetime of loving into that period. Unlike Cornelius Wyatt in Poe's short story or Benito Cereno in Melville's, Janie Crawford remembers the past *and* survives. Her memories of Tea Cake have been integrated and now form part of her own identity.

The speaker of Elizabeth Bishop's "One Art" cannot accept her loss with the same self-assurance as Janie Crawford. Bishop published "One Art" in *Geography III* (1976), her last collection of verse, a collection that takes memory as a major theme.[12] Written as a villanelle, a fixed verse form consisting of five tercets rhyming

Typically, Merwin uses no punctuation, leaving it to his readers to discern the pauses, to decide where one voice ends and another begins. The first line is John Bartram's. The poet enters at the start of the second line with a three-word tag clause identifying the initial speaker. The father then resumes his narrative, which continues over the next several stanzas.

The theme of loss enters the father's story even before he and his son discover the new plant. As the two cross some bottomland, the father notices how the river "overflows to the great / loss of those who live there": an instance of nature reclaiming its own. They soon lose their way, but this loss leads to a major find: a previously unknown species of camellia.

Once the father's narrative finishes, the poet reenters to explain that twelve years passed before the son returned. Whereas the father had discovered the species in the fall, the son rediscovered it in the spring and, therefore, had the chance to see it in bloom. The son takes over the narration for the next several stanzas. The last thing the son says is that neither he nor his father ever found "that tree growing / wild anywhere else." The poet resumes the narration to explain that the son "gathered seed and cuttings," which he planted in his own garden. The poem ends in the poet's voice, explaining what happened to the plant in its natural habitat:

> by the time he was fifty
> it had vanished from
> its own place altogether
> only surviving here and there
> as a cultivated
> foreigner

Since the appropriation of earlier literature is characteristic of much postmodern writing, Merwin's use of William Bartram's

Travels in his own *Travels* is not unusual. What is especially compelling about such appropriation is the choice of subject. The story of the discovery and disappearance of this new species appealed to Merwin for several reasons. Though the poem's title identifies the real-life father and son, nowhere does he use their names in the poem, which could be the story of any father whose son follows in his footsteps. Nor does Merwin give the scientific name for the plant, but everyone familiar with the story knows William Bartram named it in honor of Benjamin Franklin: *Franklinia alatamaha*. Omitting these proper names from the poem, Merwin prevents them from intruding on the natural tale he tells.

The father and son in "The Lost Camelia of the Bartrams" not only present a biological relationship but also represent a figurative one. William Bartram followed in his father's footsteps; William Merwin follows in the footsteps of both Bishop and Bartram. By taking cuttings from the plant, William Bartram was able to preserve the species. Edward Taylor used grafting as a metaphor; W. S. Merwin has made it part of his creative process. Borrowing from John Bartram's *Observations* and William Bartram's *Travels*, Merwin grafts their words onto his own and perpetuates them.

Much of Merwin's recent verse reflects his environmental concerns. Though relating the story of the disappearance of a species in its natural habitat, "The Lost Camelia of the Bartrams" is not about man's destruction of a species. Much as the river naturally reclaims bottomland early in the poem, nature strikes down this all-too-fragile species. Its destruction resulted from an act of nature, not of man. Many other species are lost in the same way. What makes this one different is that the Bartrams were there to bear witness to its disappearance. And the story is true. William Bartram deserves credit for collecting and cultivating the plant in his own garden. *Franklinia alatamaha* survives today solely in gardens where it is carefully tended.

The plant symbolizes memory in a number of ways. In the poem, the son takes away seed and cuttings from his exploration; these objects represent the memories we take away from any experience. We can let those memories fade or we can carefully cultivate them. There is risk in remembering, as the works of Poe and Melville demonstrate, but there is also great reward. Memory helps make us who we are. A mix of experience and emotion, memory need not destroy us; it can enhance and enrich our identities. American literature is a seedbed, a place to cultivate memory.

TIMELINE

What follows is a highly selective timeline of American literature. It lists the book-length works mentioned in the preceding text and a number of other book-length works I wanted to discuss but had neither the room nor the time to squeeze in. Dates provided are publication dates, except for works unpublished in an author's lifetime. In those cases, the dates provided are dates of composition.

1608	Captain John Smith, *A True Relation of . . . Virginia*
1616	Captain John Smith, *A Description of New England*
1620–47	William Bradford, *Of Plymouth Plantation*
1624	Captain John Smith, *The Generall Historie of Virginia, New England, and the Summer Isles*
1634	William Wood, *New Englands Prospect*
1637	Thomas Morton, *New English Canaan*
1640	*The Bay Psalm Book*
1646	Thomas Shepard, *Autobiography*
1650	Anne Bradstreet, *The Tenth Muse Lately Sprung up in America*
1666	George Alsop, *A Character of the Province of Maryland*
1672	John Josselyn, *New England's Rarities*
1678	Anne Bradstreet, *Several Poems*

1682	Mary Rowlandson, *A Narrative of the Captivity and Restoration of Mrs. Mary Rowlandson*
1689	Cotton Mather, *Right Thoughts in Sad Hours*
1702	Cotton Mather, *Magnalia Christi Americana*
1704–05	Sarah Kemble Knight, *The Journal of Madame Knight*
1705	Robert Beverley, *History of Virginia*
1708	Ebenezer Cook, *The Sot-Weed Factor*
1710	Cotton Mather, *Bonifacius* (aka *Essays to Do Good*)
1727	Cadwallader Colden, *The History of the Five Indian Nations*
1728	William Byrd II, *Secret History of the Line*
1729–47	Mark Catesby, *Natural History of Carolina, Florida, and the Bahama Islands*
1733	Benjamin Franklin, first edition of *Poor Richard's Almanack*
1736	Thomas Prince, *A Chronological History of New England*
1744	Dr Alexander Hamilton, *Itinerarium*
1751	John Bartram, *Observations*
1754	Jonathan Edwards, *Freedom of the Will*
1764	Robert Bolling, *Collection of Diverting Anecdotes*
1767	Thomas Godfrey, *The Prince of Parthia*
1771–90	Benjamin Franklin, *Autobiography*
1774	Thomas Jefferson, *A Summary View of the Rights of British America*
1776	Thomas Paine, *Common Sense*
	Thomas Jefferson, *Declaration of Independence*
1782	Hector St. John de Crèvecoeur, *Letters from an American Farmer*

(*continued*)

TIMELINE

| 1784 | Benjamin Franklin, *Information to Those Who Would Remove to America* |

1785   Thomas Jefferson, *Notes on the State of Virginia*

1787   Joel Barlow, *The Vision of Columbus*

       Royall Tyler, *The Contrast*

1787–88 Alexander Hamilton, James Madison, and John Jay, *The Federalist Papers*

1789   Olaudah Equiano, *Interesting Narrative of the Life*

1791   William Bartram, *Travels*

1798   Charles Brockden Brown, *Wieland*

1809   Washington Irving, *The History of New York*

1810   Isaiah Thomas, *The History of Printing in America*

1814   Meriwether Lewis and William Clark, *History of the Expedition Under the Command of Captains Lewis and Clark*

1817   Amasa Delano, *Narrative of Voyages and Travels*

       William Wirt, *Sketches of the Life and Character of Patrick Henry*

1819–20 Washington Irving, *The Sketch Book of Geoffrey Crayon*

1823   James Fenimore Cooper, *The Pioneers*

1824   Lydia Maria Child, *Hobomok*

1826   James Fenimore Cooper, *The Last of the Mohicans*

1827   Edgar Allan Poe, *Tamerlane and Other Poems*

1828   Nathaniel Hawthorne, *Fanshawe*

1829   Edgar Allan Poe, *Al Aaraaf, Tamerlane, and Minor Poems*

1831   Edgar Allan Poe, *Poems*

1833   Black Hawk, *The Life of Black Hawk*

(continued)

1835   Augustus Baldwin Longstreet, *Georgia Scenes*

1837   Nathaniel Hawthorne, *Twice-Told Tales*

       John Stephens, *Incidents of Travel in Egypt, Arabia Petraea, and the Holy Land*

1838   Edgar Allan Poe, *The Narrative of Arthur Gordon Pym*

1839   Edgar Allan Poe, *Tales of the Grotesque and the Arabesque*

       Nathaniel P. Willis, *Tortesa the Usurer*

1840   Richard Henry Dana, *Two Years before the Mast*

1841   James Fenimore Cooper, *The Deerslayer*

       Ralph Waldo Emerson, *Essays: First Series*

1844   Ralph Waldo Emerson, *Essays: Second Series*

       Josiah Gregg, *Commerce of the Prairies*

       George Wilkins Kendall, *Narrative of the Texan Santa Fé Expedition*

1845   Horatio Bridge, *Journal of an African Cruiser*

       Frederick Douglass, *Narrative of the Life*

       Edgar Allan Poe, *The Raven and Other Poems*

1846   Nathaniel Hawthorne, *Mosses from an Old Manse*

       Herman Melville, *Typee*

1847   Herman Melville, *Omoo*

       Osborne Russell, *Journal of a Trapper*

1849   Herman Melville, *Redburn*

       Francis Parkman, *The Oregon Trail*

       Henry David Thoreau, *A Week on the Concord and Merrimack Rivers*

(*continued*)

1850   Francis Lister Hawks, *The Monuments of Egypt*

Nathaniel Hawthorne, *The Scarlet Letter*

Herman Melville, *White-Jacket*

Donald Grant Mitchell, *The Battle Summer*

1851   Nathaniel Hawthorne, *The House of the Seven Gables*

Herman Melville, *Moby-Dick*

1852   Nathaniel Hawthorne, *The Snow-Image, and Other Twice-Told Tales*

Herman Melville, *Pierre*

Harriet Beecher Stowe, *Uncle Tom's Cabin*

1853   George W. Curtis, *The Potiphar Papers*

1854   Henry David Thoreau, *Walden*

1855   William Wells Brown, *American Fugitive in Europe*

Walt Whitman, *Leaves of Grass*

1856   John De Forest, *Oriental Acquaintance*

Matthew Calbraith Perry, *Narrative of the Expedition of an American Squadron to the China Seas and Japan*

1857   Julia Ward Howe, *Leonora*

1859   Dion Boucicault, *The Octoroon*

1860   Nathaniel Hawthorne, *The Marble Faun*

1861   Harriet Jacobs, *Incidents in the Life of a Slave Girl*

1863   Nathaniel Hawthorne, *Our Old Home*

1865   Henry David Thoreau, *The Maine Woods*

1866   Joseph Jefferson, *Rip Van Winkle*

Herman Melville, *Battle-Pieces*

(*continued*)

1867   Rebecca Harding Davis, *Waiting for the Verdict*

        George Washington Harris, *Sut Lovingood*

1868   Annie Nelles, *Life of a Book Agent*

1869   Mark Twain, *Innocents Abroad*

1870   George Kennan, *Tent Life in Siberia*

1875   Henry James, *Roderick Hudson*

        Henry James, *Transatlantic Sketches*

        John Wesley Powell, *Exploration of the Colorado River*

        Harriet Beecher Stowe, *We and Our Neighbors*

1876   Herman Melville, *Clarel*

        Mark Twain, *The Adventures of Tom Sawyer*

1877   Henry James, *The American*

1878   Henry James, *Daisy Miller*

1880   George Washington Cable, *The Grandissimes*

        Mark Twain, *A Tramp Abroad*

1881   Henry James, *The Portrait of a Lady*

1882   Lucy Bainbridge, *Round-the-World Letters*

        David Ross Locke, *Nasby in Exile*

1883   Henry James, *Portraits of Places*

1884   Helen Hunt Jackson, *Ramona*

        Henry James, *A Little Tour in France*

        Sarah Orne Jewett, *A Country Doctor*

        Florine Thayer McCray, *Wheels and Whims*

(*continued*)

TIMELINE

1885	William Dean Howells, *The Rise of Silas Lapham*
	Percival Lowell, *Chosön, The Land of the Morning Calm*
	Mark Twain, *Adventures of Huckleberry Finn*
1886	Sarah Orne Jewett, *A White Heron*
1887–88	Thomas Stevens, *Around the World on a Bicycle*
1888	Edward Bellamy, *Looking Backward*
	Herman Melville, *John Marr and Other Sailors*
1889	John Wesley Clampitt, *Echoes from the Rocky Mountains*
	Mark Twain, *A Connecticut Yankee in King Arthur's Court*
1890	Horatio Alger, *The Erie Train Boy*
	Henry James, *The Tragic Muse*
1891	George Kennan, *Siberia and the Exile System*
	Herman Melville, *Timoleon*
	Thomas Stevens, *Through Russia on a Mustang*
1893	Stephen Crane, *Maggie: A Girl of the Streets*
1895	James Lane Allen, *A Kentucky Cardinal*
	Stephen Crane, *The Black Riders*
	Stephen Crane, *The Red Badge of Courage*
1896	Sarah Orne Jewett, *The Country of the Pointed Firs*
1897	Mark Twain, *Following the Equator*
1899	Charles W. Chesnutt, *The Conjure Woman*
	Kate Chopin, *The Awakening*
	Stephen Crane, *The Monster and Other Stories*

(continued)

Stephen Crane, *War Is Kind*

Frank Norris, *McTeague*

1900   David Belasco, *Madame Butterfly*

Theodore Dreiser, *Sister Carrie*

1901   Frank Norris, *The Octopus*

1902   Henry James, *The Wings of the Dove*

1903   W. E. B. Du Bois, *The Souls of Black Folk*

Henry James, *The Ambassadors*

Jack London, *The Call of the Wild*

Frank Norris, *The Pit*

1904   Henry James, *The Golden Bowl*

1905   Edith Wharton, *The House of Mirth*

1906   Upton Sinclair, *The Jungle*

Jack London, *White Fang*

1907   Henry Adams, *The Education of Henry Adams*

Jack London, *The Road*

1908   Frederick Dellenbaugh, *A Canyon Voyage*

1910   Jane Addams, *Twenty Years at Hull House*

1911   Rachel Crothers, *He and She*

Theodore Dreiser, *Jennie Gerhardt*

Edith Wharton, *Ethan Frome*

David Graham Phillips, *The Husband's Story*

1913   Willa Cather, *O Pioneers!*

Robert Frost, *A Boy's Will*

(continued)

1914	Willa Cather, [Samuel McClure's] *My Autobiography*
	Robert Frost, *North of Boston*
1917	T. S. Eliot, *Prufrock and Other Observations*
	Hamlin Garland, *A Son of the Middle Border*
	David Graham Phillips, *Susan Lenox*
	Upton Sinclair, *King Coal*
1918	Willa Cather, *My Antonia*
1920	F. Scott Fitzgerald, *This Side of Paradise*
	Sinclair Lewis, *Main Street*
	Eugene O'Neill, *Beyond the Horizon*
	Edith Wharton, *The Age of Innocence*
1921	Eugene O'Neill, *Anna Christie*
1922	T. S. Eliot, *The Wasteland*
	F. Scott Fitzgerald, *The Beautiful and the Damned*
1923	William Carlos Williams, *The Great American Novel*
	Wallace Stevens, *Harmonium*
1924	Ernest Hemingway, *In Our Time*
1925	H. D., *Collected Poems*
	John Dos Passos, *Manhattan Transfer*
	Theodore Dreiser, *An American Tragedy*
	F. Scott Fitzgerald, *The Great Gatsby*
	Anita Loos, *Gentlemen Prefer Blondes*
	Ezra Pound, *A Draft of XVI Cantos*
	William Carlos Williams, *In the American Grain*

(*continued*)

1926   Ernest Hemingway, *The Sun Also Rises*

1927   Willa Cather, *Death Comes for the Archbishop*

       Ernest Hemingway, *Men Without Women*

1928   Major Taylor, *The Fastest Bicycle Rider in the World*

1929   William Faulkner, *The Sound and the Fury*

       Thomas Wolfe, *Look Homeward, Angel*

1930   Hart Crane, *The Bridge*

       John Dos Passos, *The 42nd Parallel*

       William Faulkner, *As I Lay Dying*

       Robert Sherwood, *Waterloo Bridge*

1931   William Faulkner, *The Hamlet*

       Eugene O'Neill, *Mourning Becomes Electra*

1932   John Do Passos, *1919*

       William Faulkner, *Light in August*

       Frank Lloyd Wright, *Autobiography*

1934   James M. Cain, *The Postman Always Rings Twice*

       F. Scott Fitzgerald, *Tender Is the Night*

       Langston Hughes, *The Ways of White Folks*

       Henry Miller, *Tropic of Cancer*

       Ezra Pound, *Eleven New Cantos*

1935   Ernest Hemingway, *Green Hills of Africa*

       Horace McCoy, *They Shoot Horses, Don't They?*

1936   Louis Armstrong, *Swing that Music*

(*continued*)

John Dos Passos, *The Big Money*

William Faulkner, *Absalom, Absalom!*

1937   Charles Eliot Goodspeed, *Yankee Bookseller*

Ernest Hemingway, *To Have and Have Not*

Zora Neale Hurston, *Their Eyes Were Watching God*

Younghill Kang, *East Goes West*

1938   John Dos Passos, *U.S.A.*

1939   Raymond Chandler, *The Big Sleep*

Ernest Hemingway, *The First Forty-Nine Stories*

Eugene O'Neill, *The Iceman Cometh*

John Steinbeck, *The Grapes of Wrath*

Nathanael West, *The Day of the Locust*

1940   Raymond Chandler, *Farewell, My Lovely*

Ernest Hemingway, *For Whom the Bell Tolls*

Carson McCullers, *The Heart Is a Lonely Hunter*

Richard Wright, *Native Son*

1941   W. C. Handy, *Father of the Blues*

Theodore Roethke, *Open House*

John Steinbeck, *Sea of Cortez*

1942   William Faulkner, *Go Down, Moses*

Zora Neale Hurston, *Dust Tracks on a Road*

1943   T. S. Eliot, *Four Quartets*

Woody Guthrie, *Bound for Glory*

Salom Rizk, *Syrian Yankee*

(continued)

1945   John Steinbeck, *Cannery Row*

        Tennessee Williams, *The Glass Menagerie*

        Richard Wright, *Black Boy*

1946   Elizabeth Bishop, *North and South*

        Eugene O'Neill, *The Iceman Cometh*

1946–58 William Carlos Williams, *Paterson*

1947   Tennessee Williams, *A Streetcar Named Desire*

1948   Norman Mailer, *The Naked and the Dead*

        Theodore Roethke, *The Lost Son and Other Poems*

        John Steinbeck, *A Russian Journal*

        Cornell Woolrich, *I Married a Dead Man*

1949   Arthur Miller, *Death of a Salesman*

        Claude Shannon, *Mathematical Theory of Communication*

1950   Jelly Roll Morton, *Mister Jelly Roll*

1951   Langston Hughes, *Montage of a Dream Deferred*

        Carson McCullers, *Ballad of the Sad Café*

        J. D. Salinger, *The Catcher in the Rye*

        William Carlos Williams, *Autobiography*

1952   Ralph Ellison, *Invisible Man*

        Ernest Hemingway, *The Old Man and the Sea*

        Lillian Ross, *Picture*

1953   Paddy Chayefsky, *Marty*

1954   Louis Armstrong, *Satchmo*

        Daniel Hoffman, *An Armada of Thirty Whales*

(*continued*)

1955	Elizabeth Bishop, *Poems*
	William Gaddis, *The Recognitions*
	Arthur Miller, *A View from the Bridge*
	Flannery O'Connor, *A Good Man Is Hard to Find, and Other Stories*
1956	Allen Ginsberg, *Howl and Other Poems*
	Billie Holiday, *Lady Sings the Blues*
1957	William Faulkner, *The Town*
	Jack Kerouac, *On the Road*
	Denise Levertov, *Here and Now*
1958	Jack Kerouac, *The Dharma Bums*
	Jack Kerouac, *The Subterraneans*
	Vladimir Nabokov, *Lolita*
1959	William Burroughs, *Naked Lunch*
	William Faulkner, *The Mansion*
1960	Sidney Bechet, *Treat It Gentle*
	John Barth, *The Sot-Weed Factor*
	W. S. Merwin, *The Drunk in the Furnace*
1961	Joseph Heller, *Catch-22*
	Richard Hugo, *A Run of Jacks*
	Bernard Malamud, *The Natural*
	Tennessee Williams, *The Night of the Iguana*
	Richard Wright, *Eight Men*
1962	Edward Albee, *Who's Afraid of Virginia Woolf?*
	Ken Kesey, *One Flew over the Cuckoo's Nest*

(*continued*)

Vladimir Nabokov, *Pale Fire*

John Steinbeck, *Travels with Charley*

1963 Sylvia Plath, *The Bell Jar*

Thomas Pynchon, *V*

Richard Wright, *The Branch Will Not Break*

1964 Paddy Chayefsky, *The Americanization of Emily*

Ken Kesey, *Sometimes a Great Notion*

1965 Donald Barthelme, *Snow White*

Elizabeth Bishop, *Questions of Travel*

Norman Mailer, *An American Dream*

1966 Truman Capote, *In Cold Blood*

Sylvia Plath, *Ariel*

Thomas Pynchon, *The Crying of Lot 49*

1967 Sam Shepard, *Forensic and the Navigators*

Hunter S. Thompson, *Hell's Angels*

1968 Joan Didion, *Slouching Towards Bethlehem*

Norman Mailer, *The Armies of the Night*

Philip Roth, *Portnoy's Complaint*

James Watson, *The Double Helix*

Tom Wolfe, *The Electric Kool-Aid Acid Test*

1969 John Berryman, *Dream Songs*

Cecil Brown, *The Life and Loves of Mr. Jiveass Nigger*

Charles Gordone, *No Place to Be Somebody*

(continued)

Sam Greenlee, *The Spook Who Sat by the Door*

Ezra Pound, *Drafts and Fragments of Cantos CX–CXVII*

1970   James Dickey, *Deliverance*

Jake La Motta, *Raging Bull*

Toni Morrison, *The Bluest Eye*

1971   Paddy Chayefsky, *The Hospital*

Charles Mingus, *Beneath the Underdog*

Gay Talese, *Honor Thy Father*

Hunter S. Thompson, *Fear and Loathing in Las Vegas*

1973   Peter Maas, *Serpico*

Philip Roth, *The Great American Novel*

1975   Paul Theroux, *The Great Railway Bazaar*

1976   Elizabeth Bishop, *Geography III*

Raymond Carver, *Will You Please Be Quiet, Please?*

Paddy Chayefsky, *Network*

Maxine Hong Kingston, *The Woman Warrior*

1977   Richard Hugo, *31 Letters and 13 Dreams*

Toni Morrison, *Song of Solomon*

1978   Gibbons Ruark, *Reeds*

1979   Richard Hugo, *The Triggering Town*

Paul Theroux, *The Old Patagonian Express*

Tom Wolfe, *The Right Stuff*

1980   Maxine Hong Kingston, *China Men*

1981   Raymond Carver, *What We Talk About When We Talk About Love*

(continued)

1982	Theresa Hak Kyung Cha, *Dictee*
1983	Paul Theroux, *The Kingdom by the Sea*
1984	Raymond Carver, *Cathedral*
	Sandra Cisneros, *The House on Mango Street*
1985	Count Basie, *Good Morning Blues*
	Cormac McCarthy, *Blood Meridian*
	August Wilson, *Fences*
1987	Tom Wolfe, *The Bonfire of the Vanities*
1988	Daniel Hoffman, *Hang-Gliding from Helicon*
1989	Miles Davis, *Miles*
	Maxine Hong Kingston, *Tripmaster Monkey*
1990	August Wilson, *The Piano Lesson*
1991	Edward Albee, *Three Tall Women*
1993	W. S. Merwin, *Travels*
1995	Chang-rae Lee, *Native Speaker*
1998	Tom Wolfe, *A Man in Full*
1999	Jhumpa Lahiri, *Interpreter of Maladies*
2000	Brian Hayes, *A Boy Scout in Hollywood*
2001	Jonathan Franzen, *The Corrections*
	Quincy Jones, *Q*
2003	Jhumpa Lahiri, *The Namesake*
2004	Bob Dylan, *Chronicles*
	Philip Roth, *The Plot against America*

(continued)

TIMELINE

Tom Wolfe, *I Am Charlotte Simmons*

2005   T. Coraghessan Boyle, *Tooth and Claw*

W. S. Merwin, *Summer Doorways*

2006   Natasha Trethewey, *Native Guard*

2010   Jonathan Franzen, *Freedom*

NOTES

Chapter 1: "Beginnings"

1. Priscilla L. Walton, *Our Cannibals, Ourselves* (Urbana: University of Illinois Press, 2004), 19–20.
2. Terry Southern, *Now Dig This: The Unspeakable Writings of Terry Southern, 1950–1995,* ed. Niles Southern and Josh Alan Friedman (New York: Grove Press, 2001), 191–94.
3. Joel Coen and Ethan Coen, *Blood Simple* (London: Faber and Faber, 1996), viii.
4. Kevin J. Hayes, *The Cambridge Introduction to Herman Melville* (New York: Cambridge University Press, 2007), 46–48.
5. Allen Ginsberg, *Deliberate Prose: Selected Essays, 1952–1995,* ed. Bill Morgan (New York: HarperCollins, 2000), 301.
6. Toni Morrison, *What Moves at the Margin: Selected Nonfiction,* ed. Carolyn C. Denard (Jackson: University Press of Mississippi, 2008), 65.
7. Quoted in Michael Palin, *Diaries 1969–1979: The Python Years* (New York: Thomas Dunne Books/St. Martin's Press, 2007), 529.
8. Philip Roth, *Conversations with Philip Roth,* ed. George J. Searles (Jackson: University Press of Mississippi, 1992), 120.
9. Elaine B. Safer, *Mocking the Age: The Later Novels of Philip Roth* (Albany: State University of New York Press, 2006), 153.
10. Sam Shepard, *The Unseen Hand and Other Plays* (1972; reprinted, New York: Urizen Books, 1981), 56.
11. John Smith, *The Complete Works of Captain John Smith (1580–1631),* ed. Philip L. Barbour (Chapel Hill: University of North Carolina Press, 1986), 1:343. This quotation and others from Smith have been slightly modernized for clarity.

12. Ibid., 1:330.
13. Kevin J. Hayes, "How Thomas Prince Read Captain John Smith," in *Finding Colonial Americas: Essays Honoring J. A. Leo Lemay*, ed. Carla Mulford and David S. Shields (Newark: University of Delaware Press, 2001), 376.
14. Charles Olson, *Collected Prose*, ed. Donald Allen and Benjamin Friedlander (Berkeley: University of California Press, 1997), 320.
15. For a discussion of the use of negative catalogues, see Terence Martin, "The Negative Structures of American Literature," *American Literature* 57 (1985): 1–22.
16. Smith, *Complete Works*, 1:332.
17. Ibid., 1:347.
18. Benjamin Franklin, *Writings*, ed. J. A. Leo Lemay (New York: Library of America, 1987), 978.
19. Thomas Jefferson, *The Papers of Thomas Jefferson*, ed. Julian P. Boyd et al. (Princeton: Princeton University Press, 1950–), 1:122–23.
20. J. Hector St. John de Crèvecoeur, *Letters from an American Farmer and Sketches of Eighteenth-Century America*, ed. Albert E. Stone (New York: Penguin, 1981), 67.
21. Ibid., 70.
22. David Graham Phillips, *The Husband's Story: A Novel* (New York: D. Appleton, 1911), 82; Phillips, *Susan Lenox: Her Fall and Rise* (1917; reprinted, Carbondale: Southern Illinois University Press, 1977), 1:411.
23. Horatio Alger Jr., *The Erie Train Boy* (1890; reprinted, New York: Hurst, 1900), 145.
24. Christopher Lehmann-Haupt, "Heinous Chemicals at Work," *New York Times*, June 22, 1972, 37.
25. Ralph Ellison, *Invisible Man* (1952; reprinted, New York: Vintage, 1995), 111; Hunter S. Thompson, *Fear and Loathing in Las Vegas: A Savage Journey into the Heart of the American Dream* (New York: Popular Library, 1971), 70.
26. Ellison, *Invisible Man*, 108; Phillips, *Susan Lenox*, 2:147.
27. Florine Thayer McCray, *Wheels and Whims: An Etching* (Boston: Cupples, Upham, 1884), 203.
28. [Charles Brockden Brown,] "Memoirs of Stephen Calvert," *Monthly Magazine* 2 (January 1800): 26.
29. Ralph Waldo Emerson, *Essays and Lectures*, ed. Joel Porte (New York: Library of America, 1983), 259, 261.
30. Henry David Thoreau, *A Week on the Concord and Merrimack Rivers*, ed. Carl Hovde (Princeton: Princeton University Press, 1980), 188.
31. Henry David Thoreau, *The Maine Woods*, ed. Joseph J. Moldenhauer (Princeton: Princeton University Press, 1982), 14.
32. Ibid., 69, 71.

Chapter 2 : "Travels"

1. Sarah Kemble Knight, *The Private Journal of a Journey from Boston to New York in the Year 1704*, ed. William Law Learned (Albany: F. H. Little, 1865), 20.
2. Ibid., 21, 27. The last quotation has been slightly modernized for clarity.
3. Donald Grant Mitchell, *The Works of Donald G. Mitchell* (New York: Charles Scribner's Sons, 1907), 14:64.
4. William Byrd II, *William Byrd's Histories of the Dividing Line Betwixt Virginia and North Carolina*, ed. William K. Boyd (1929; reprinted, New York: Dover, 1967), 317.
5. Ibid., 288.
6. Kevin J. Hayes, "A Colonial American Masterwork," *Resources in American Literary Study* 19 (1993): 296.
7. For a detailed literary assessment, see Thomas Hallock, "Narrative, Nature, and Cultural Contact in John Bartram's *Observations*," in *America's Curious Botanist: A Tercentennial Reappraisal of John Bartram, 1699–1777*, ed. Nancy E. Hoffmann and John C. Van Horne (Philadelphia: American Philosophical Society, 2004), 107–25.
8. James Dickey, "Introduction," *Travels Through North and South Carolina, Georgia, East and West Florida, The Cherokee Country, the Extensive Territories of the Muscogulges, or Creek Confederacy, and the Country of the Chactaws* (New York: Penguin, 1988), viii.
9. John Livingston Lowes, *The Road to Xanadu: A Study in the Ways of the Imagination* (1927; reprinted, Boston: Houghton Mifflin, 1955), 287–88, 332–35, 409.
10. Quoted in Joseph Sabin, *Catalogue of the Books, Manuscripts, and Engravings Belonging to William Menzies of New York* (New York, 1875), 151.
11. George W. Kendall, *Narrative of the Texan Santa Fé Expedition* (London: Henry Washbourne, 1847), 1.
12. Charles Dudley Warner, *Captain John Smith* (New York: Henry Holt, 1881), 191.
13. Osborne Russell, *Journal of a Trapper*, ed. Aubrey L. Haines (1955; reprinted, Lincoln: University of Nebraska Press, 1965), 38.
14. Herman Melville, *The Piazza Tales and Other Prose Pieces, 1839–1860*, ed. Harrison Hayford, Alma A. MacDougall, and G. Thomas Tanselle (Evanston, IL: Northwestern University Press and the Newberry Library, 1987), 233.
15. Frederick S. Dellenbaugh, *A Canyon Voyage: The Narrative of the Second Powell Expedition down the Green-Colorado River from Wyoming, and the Explorations on Land in the Years 1871 and 1872* (1908; reprinted, Tucson: University of Arizona Press, 1996).

16. J. A. Leo Lemay, *"New England's Annoyances": America's First Folk Song* (Newark: University of Delaware Press, 1985), 18.

17. Henry James, *Literary Criticism*, ed. Leon Edel (New York: Library of America, 1984), 432.

18. Harold F. Smith, *American Travellers Abroad: A Bibliography of Accounts Published Before 1900*, 2nd ed. (Lanham, MD: Scarecrow Press, 1999), 325–26.

19. John Lloyd Stephens, *Incidents of Travel in Egypt, Arabia Petraea, and the Holy Land*, ed. Victor Wolfgang von Hagen (1970; reprinted, San Francisco: Chronicle Books, 1991), 153.

20. Herman Melville, *Redburn, His First Voyage: Being the Sailor-Boy Confessions and Reminiscences of the Son-of-a-Gentleman, in the Merchant Service*, ed. Harrison Hayford, Hershel Parker, and G. Thomas Tanselle (Evanston, IL: Northwestern University Press and the Newberry Library, 1969), 5.

21. For an excellent study of this series, see Ezra Greenspan, "Evert Duyckinck and the History of Wiley and Putnam's Library of American Books, 1845–1847," *American Literature* 64 (1992): 677–93.

22. Frederick S. Dellenbaugh, "Travellers and Explorers, 1846–1900," in *The Cambridge History of American Literature*, ed. William Peterfield Trent et al. (1921; reprinted, New York: Macmillan, 1933), 1:156.

23. Henry James, *Collected Travel Writings: The Continent*, ed. Richard Howard (New York: Library of America, 1993), 88.

24. "Among the Books," *Outing and the Wheelman* 5 (November 1884): 143.

25. Thomas Stevens, *Around the World on a Bicycle* (London: Sampson, Low, Marston, Searle, and Rivington, 1887), 1:114.

26. Douglas Brinkley, "A Depression Project That Gave Rise to a Generation of Novelists," *New York Times*, August 2, 2003, B7.

27. *The Ohio Guide* (New York: Oxford University Press, 1940), 325.

28. John Steinbeck, *Travels with Charley: In Search of America* (New York: Penguin, 1997), 103.

Chapter 3 : "Autobiography"

1. Kevin J. Hayes, "Benjamin Franklin," in *The Oxford Handbook to Early American Literature*, ed. Kevin J. Hayes (New York: Oxford University Press, 2008), 443–44.

2. Tom Wolfe, "Appendices to the Foregoing Work," *Esquire* 78 (December 1972): 274.

3. Thomas Shepard, *God's Plot: The Paradoxes of Puritan Piety, Being the Autobiography and Journal of Thomas Shepard*, ed. Michael McGiffert (Amherst: University of Massachusetts Press, 1972), 41.

4. Shepard, *God's Plot*, 60.
5. Frederick Douglass, *Narrative of the Life of Frederick Douglass, An American Slave*, ed., Benjamin Quarles (Cambridge, MA: Belknap Press, 1988), 23.
6. Wolfgang Mieder, "'Do Unto Others as You Would Have Them Do Unto You': Frederick Douglass's Proverbial Struggle for Civil Rights," *Journal of American Folklore* 114 (2001): 331–57.
7. Douglass, *Narrative*, 57.
8. Ibid., 58.
9. James Walvin, "Equiano, Olaudah," in *Oxford Dictionary of National Biography*, ed. H. C. G. Matthew and Brian Harrison (New York: Oxford University Press, 2004).
10. Bob Dylan, *Chronicles* (New York: Simon and Schuster, 2004), 245.
11. Quoted in Robert Thacker, "Introduction," *The Autobiography of S. S. McClure*, by Willa Cather (Lincoln: University of Nebraska Press, 1997), v.
12. Martin Scorsese, *Interviews*, ed. Peter Brunette (Jackson: University Press of Mississippi, 1999), 85.
13. Jake La Motta, Joseph Carter, and Peter Savage, *Raging Bull* (1970; reprinted, New York: Bantam, 1980), 1.
14. La Motta, Carter, and Savage, *Raging Bull*, 15.
15. For further discussions of this newly defined genre, see Christopher Harlos, "Jazz Autobiography: Theory, Practice, Politics," in *Representing Jazz*, ed. Krin Gabbard (Durham: Duke University Press, 1995), 131–66; Jürgen E. Grandt, *Kinds of Blue: The Jazz Aesthetic in African American Narrative* (Columbus: Ohio State University Press, 2004); and Holly E. Farrington, "Narrating the Jazz Life: Three Approaches in Jazz Autobiography," *Popular Music and Society* 29 (2006): 375–86.
16. Alan Lomax, "Preface to the 1973 Edition," *Mister Jelly Roll: The Fortunes of Jelly Roll Morton, New Orleans Creole and "Inventor of Jazz,"* ed. Alan Lomax (Berkeley: University of California Press, 2001), xv.
17. Quincy Troupe, "Afterword," *Miles: The Autobiography*, by Miles Davis and Quincy Troupe (1989; reprinted, New York: Simon and Schuster, 2005), 415.
18. David Ake, *Jazz Matters: Sound, Place, and Time Since Bebop* (Berkeley: University of California, 2010), 56–58.
19. Quincy Jones, *Q: The Autobiography of Quincy Jones* (New York: Doubleday, 2001), 157.
20. Robert Frost, *Collected Poems, Prose, and Plays*, ed. Richard Poirier and Mark Richardson (New York: Library of America, 1995), 275.
21. James D. Watson, *The Double Helix: A Personal Account of the Discovery of the Structure of DNA*, ed. Gunther S. Stent (New York: Norton, 1980), 24.
22. Ibid., 131.
23. "Notes of a Not-Watson (1968)," in *Double Helix*, 179.

Chapter 4 : "Narrative Voice and the Short Story"

1. Washington Irving, *History, Tales and Sketches*, ed. James W. Tuttleton (New York: Library of America, 1983), 781.
2. Nathaniel Hawthorne, *The Snow Image and Uncollected Tales*, ed. William Charvat (Columbus: Ohio State University Press, 1974), 231.
3. John Tresch, "Extra! Extra! Poe Invents Science Fiction!" in *The Cambridge Companion to Edgar Allan Poe*, ed. Kevin J. Hayes (New York: Cambridge University Press, 2002), 113–32.
4. For a detailed treatment of the subject, see James H. Justus, *Fetching the Old Southwest: Humorous Writing from Longstreet to Twain* (Columbia: University of Missouri Press, 2004).
5. Augustus Baldwin Longstreet, *Georgia Scenes: Characters, Incidents, etc., in the First Half-Century of the Republic* (1840; reprinted, New York: Harper and Brothers, 1897), iii.
6. Ibid., 70.
7. Ibid., 78.
8. For a thorough critical appreciation, see J. A. Leo Lemay, "The Text, Tradition, and Themes of 'The Big Bear of Arkansas,'" *American Literature* 47 (1975): 321–42.
9. For the text of "The Bear," a series of pertinent documents, and several perceptive critical essays, see Francis Lee Utley, Lynn Z. Bloom, and Arthur F. Kinney, eds. *Bear, Man, God: Seven Approaches to William Faulkner's "The Bear"* (New York: Random House, 1964).
10. George W. Harris, *Sut Lovingood: Yarns Spun by a "Nat'ral Born Durn'd Fool"* (New York: Dick and Fitzgerald, 1867), 198.
11. Ernest Hemingway, *Green Hills of Africa* (New York: Charles Scribner's Sons, 1935), 22.
12. Ralph Ellison, *The Collected Essays of Ralph Ellison*, ed. John F. Callahan (New York: Modern Library, 2003), 123.
13. Kevin J. Hayes, *Stephen Crane* (Tavistock: Northcote House, 2003), 67–69.
14. Ernest Hemingway, *The Short Stories of Ernest Hemingway* (New York: Charles Scribner's Sons, 1953), 355.
15. Richard Wright, *Eight Men* (Cleveland: World, 1961), 11.
16. Cecil Brown, "The Lesson and the Legacy," *Negro Digest* 18 (December 1968): 50.
17. Cecil Brown, *The Life and Loves of Mr. Jiveass Nigger: A Novel* (1969; reprinted, New York: Ecco Press, 1991), 22.
18. Wright, *Eight Men*, 26.
19. Flannery O'Connor, *Collected Works*, ed. Sally Fitzgerald (New York: Library of America, 1988), 283.

20. Quoted in Dinitia Smith, "Gaddis in the Details: Is America Finally Ready for the Literary Wizard of the Hamptons?" *New York*, January 3, 1994, 38.

21. Thomas Pynchon, "Entropy," in *The Norton Anthology of American Literature, Volume E: Literature Since 1945*, ed. Jerome Klinkowitz and Patricia B. Wallace, 7th ed. (New York: Norton, 2007), 2823.

22. Sandra Cisneros, "Woman Hollering Creek," *Norton Anthology*, 3170.

Chapter 5 : *"Poetry"*

1. Walt Whitman, *Complete Poetry and Collected Prose*, ed. Justin Kaplan (New York: Library of America, 1982), 287–97.

2. Ibid., 656.

3. Emily Dickinson, *Poems: Including Variant Readings Critically Compared with All Known Manuscripts*, ed. Thomas H. Johnson (Cambridge, MA: Belknap Press, 1955), 1:206–7.

4. Kevin J. Hayes, "Poe, the Daguerreotype, and the Autobiographical Act," *Biography* 25 (2002): 477–92.

5. Herman Melville to Evert A. Duyckinck, February 12, 1851, in *Correspondence*, ed. Lynn Horth (Evanston, IL: Northwestern University Press and the Newberry Library, 1993), 180.

6. David Haven Blake, *Walt Whitman and the Culture of Celebrity* (New Haven: Yale University Press, 2006), 46.

7. Dickinson, *Poems*, 1:544.

8. Anne Bradstreet, *The Works of Anne Bradstreet in Prose and Verse*, ed. John Harvard Ellis (Charlestown: Abram E. Cutter, 1867), 389.

9. George Alsop, *A Character of the Province of Maryland*, ed. John Gilmary Shea (New York: William Gowans, 1869), 26.

10. Thomas H. Johnson, "Taylor's Library," in *The Poetical Works of Edward Taylor*, ed. Thomas H. Johnson (1939; reprinted, Princeton: Princeton University Press, 1971), 212. For supplementary information on Taylor's library, see Kevin J. Hayes, "Portraits of the Mind: Ebenezer Devotion and Ezra Stiles," *New England Quarterly* 70 (1997): 624.

11. Taylor, *Poetical Works*, 140.

12. Robert Bolling, "Neanthe," in *American Poetry: The Seventeenth and Eighteenth Centuries*, ed. David S. Shields (New York: Library of America, 2007), 628.

13. J. A. Leo Lemay, "Southern Colonial Grotesque: Robert Bolling's 'Neanthe,'" *Mississippi Quarterly* 35 (1982): 97–126.

14. For the fullest bibliography of printed early American verse, see J. A. Leo Lemay, *A Calendar of American Poetry in the Colonial Newspapers and Magazines and in the Major English Magazines Through 1765* (Worcester, MA: American Antiquarian Society, 1972).

15. Kevin J. Hayes, *Edgar Allan Poe* (London: Reaktion, 2009), 9–10.
16. Herman Melville, *The Works of Herman Melville*, ed. Michael Sadleir (London: Constable, 1922–24), 16:23.
17. Kevin J. Hayes, *The Cambridge Introduction to Herman Melville* (New York: Cambridge University Press, 2007), 91.
18. Amy Lowell, "Introduction," in *The Works of Stephen Crane*, ed. Wilson Follett (New York: Knopf, 1925), 6:x.
19. Stephen Crane, *The Black Riders and Other Lines* (Boston: Copeland and Day, 1896), xi.
20. Kevin J. Hayes, *Stephen Crane* (Tavistock, UK: Northcote House, 2003), 30–31.
21. Stephen Crane, *The University of Virginia Edition of the Works of Stephen Crane*, ed. Fredson Bowers (Charlottesville: University Press of Virginia, 1969–76), 10:52.
22. T. S. Eliot, *The Complete Poems and Plays, 1909–1950* (San Diego: Harcourt Brace Jovanovich, 1971), 16.
23. Hayes, *Stephen Crane*, 31.
24. Eliot, *Complete Poems*, 130.
25. T. S. Eliot, *The Waste Land: A Facsimile and Transcript of the Original Drafts Including the Annotations of Ezra Pound* (New York: Harcourt Brace Jovanovich, 1971).
26. Ezra Pound, *Literary Essays of Ezra Pound*, ed. T. S. Eliot (New York: New Directions, 1968), 382.
27. Wallace Stevens, *Collected Poetry and Prose*, ed. Frank Kermode and Joan Richardson (New York: Library of America, 1997), 76.
28. Ibid., 311–12.
29. Sylvia Plath, *Ariel* (New York: Harper and Row, 1966), 49–52.
30. Richard Hugo, *The Triggering Town: Lectures and Essays on Poetry and Writing* (New York: Norton, 1979), 27.
31. Ibid., 14.
32. Ibid., 5.

Chapter 6 : "The Drama of the Everyday"

1. George Jean Nathan, *The Theatre, the Drama, the Girls* (New York: Knopf, 1921), 181.
2. Eugene O'Neill, *Complete Plays*, ed. Travis Bogard (New York: Library of America, 1988), 1:968.
3. Kevin J. Hayes, "Prostitution," in *American History Through Literature, 1870–1920*, ed. Tom Quirk and Gary Scharnhorst (New York: Charles Scribner's Sons, 2006), 3:914–16.

4. O'Neill, *Complete Plays*, 1:1007, 1023.

5. Ibid., 3:610, 629.

6. Raymond Chandler to Cleve Adams, September 4, 1948, in *Selected Letters of Raymond Chandler*, ed. Frank MacShane (New York: Columbia University Press, 1981), 126–27.

7. Arthur Miller, *The Portable Arthur Miller*, ed. Christopher Bigsby (New York: Viking Press, 2003), 81.

8. Ibid., 60.

9. Arthur Miller, "Tragedy and the Common Man," *New York Times*, February 27, 1949, X1.

10. Herman Melville, *Moby-Dick: or, The Whale*, ed. Harrison Hayford, Hershel Parker, and G. Thomas Tanselle (Evanston, IL: Northwestern University Press and the Newberry Library, 1988), 117.

11. Tennessee Williams, *A Streetcar Named Desire* (1947; reprinted, New York: New Directions, 1980), 12.

12. Sam Peckinpah, *Interviews*, ed. Kevin J. Hayes (Jackson: University Press of Mississippi, 2008), 111.

13. David S. [Sam] Peckinpah, "An Analysis of the Method Used in Producing and Directing a One Act Play for the Stage and for a Closed Circuit Television Broadcast," M.A. thesis, University of Southern California, 1954, 12.

14. Peckinpah, *Interviews*, 111.

15. Neal Conan, "Playwright Edward Albee Discusses His Career and the Production of His Latest Play, *The Goat: or, Who Is Sylvia?*" *Talk of the Nation*, National Public Radio, March 6, 2002.

16. Quoted in Jean Vallely, "The James Garner Files," *Esquire*, July 3–19, 1979, 73.

17. Christopher Wicking and Tise Vahimagi, *The American Vein: Directors and Directions in Television* (New York: E. P. Dutton, 1979), 54.

Chapter 7 : "The Great American Novel"

1. Maxine Hong Kingston, "The Novel's Next Step," *Mother Jones*, October 1989, 39.

2. Henry James, *Literary Criticism*, ed. Leon Edel (New York: Library of America, 1984), 221.

3. John W. DeForest, "The Great American Novel," *Nation* 6 (January 9, 1868): 28.

4. Rebecca Harding Davis, "Women in Literature," *Independent* 43 (May 7, 1891): 1–2.

5. James Lane Allen, "The Great American Novel," *Independent* 43 (September 24, 1891): 3–4.

6. [William Morton Payne,] "The Great American Novel," *Dial* 21 (December 1, 1896): 317–19.

7. Frank Norris, *Novels and Essays*, ed. Donald Pizer (New York: Library of America, 1986), 1181.

8. Ibid., 1181–2.

9. "The Great American Novel," *Globe* [New York], July 2, 1918.

10. Ezra Pound, *Literary Essays of Ezra Pound*, ed. T. S. Eliot (New York: New Directions, 1968), 395.

11. William Carlos Williams, *The Autobiography of William Carlos Williams* (New York: Random House, 1951), 237.

12. Edith Wharton, "The Great American Novel," *Yale Review*, n.s., 16 (July 1927): 647.

13. Ibid., 653.

14. Ibid., "Great American Novel," 654.

15. F. Scott Fitzgerald, *The Great Gatsby* (1925; reprinted, New York: Scribner's, 1953), 177.

16. Ibid., 99.

17. Jean Stein Vanden Heuvel, "William Faulkner," in *Writers at Work: The Paris Review Interviews, First Series*, ed. Malcolm Cowley (New York: Penguin, 1979), 134.

18. Joseph Heller, *Conversations with Joseph Heller*, ed. Adam J. Sorkin (Jackson: University Press of Mississippi, 1993), 68.

19. Ken Kesey, *Sometimes a Great Notion* (1964; reprinted, New York: Penguin, 2006), 79.

20. Donald Barthelme, *Snow White* (1965; reprinted, New York: Simon and Schuster, 1996), 65.

21. Tom Wolfe, "Why They Aren't Writing the Great American Novel Anymore," *Esquire*, December 1972, 157.

22. Kingston, "The Novel's Next Step," 40.

23. Lev Grossman, "Jonathan Franzen: The Wide Shot," *Time*, August 23, 2010, 46.

Chapter 8 : "Endings"

1. J. Hector St. John de Crèvecoeur, *Letters from an American Farmer and Sketches of Eighteenth-Century America*, ed. Albert E. Stone (New York: Penguin, 1981), 67.

2. Henry James, *Novels, 1871–1880*, ed. William T. Stafford (New York: Library of America, 1983), 872.

3. Kevin J. Hayes, ed., *Henry James: The Contemporary Reviews* (New York: Cambridge University Press, 1996), 28.

4. Edgar Allan Poe, *Collected Works of Edgar Allan Poe*, ed. Thomas Ollive Mabbott (Cambridge, MA: Belknap Press, 1969–78), 3:969.

5. Ibid., 3:969.

6. Herman Melville, *The Piazza Tales and Other Prose Pieces, 1839–1860*, ed. Harrison Hayford, Alma A. MacDougall, and G. Thomas Tanselle (Evanston, IL: Northwestern University Press and the Newberry Library, 1987), 48.

7. Quoted in Jay Leyda, *The Melville Log: A Documentary Life of Herman Melville, 1819–1891* (1951; reprinted, New York: Gordian Press, 1969), 2:500–1.

8. Melville, *Piazza Tales*, 116.

9. Zora Neale Hurston, *Novels and Stories*, ed. Cheryl A. Wall (New York: Library of America, 1995), 332.

10. Zora Neale Hurston, *Folklore, Memoirs, and Other Writings*, ed. Cheryl A. Wall (New York: Library of America, 1995), 583.

11. Hurston, *Novels and Stories*, 333.

12. Elizabeth Bishop, *Poems, Prose, and Letters*, ed. Robert Giroux and Lloyd Schwartz (New York: Library of America, 2008).

13. W. S. Merwin, "Lament for the Makers," in *Lament for the Makers: A Memorial Anthology*, ed. W. S. Merwin (Washington, DC: Counterpoint, 1996), 11.

14. W. S. Merwin, *Travels* (New York: Knopf, 1994), 38–40.

FURTHER READING

Everyone interested in American literature should look to the Library of America for further reading. First established in 1979, the Library of America has attempted to publish the best and most significant works in American literary history. These handsome, finely printed, generally authoritative editions form the fullest collection of American literature ever assembled. Most of the literary quotations in the present work come from various Library of America editions.

Biographical dictionaries are the best places to start for further information about writers discussed here. Oxford University Press publishes the two most pertinent and authoritative multivolume works: *American National Biography* (1999) or *ANB*, edited by John A. Garraty and Mark C. Carnes, and *Oxford Dictionary of National Biography* (2004) or *ODNB*, edited by H. C. G. Matthew and Brian Harrison. Though the latter work is a collection of British biography, its editors cast a wide net, so many figures from early American literature are included. *The Dictionary of Literary Biography* (1978–) or *DLB* and *Contemporary Authors* (1962–) provide additional biographical information, especially for more recent authors. All of these references are available in hard copy or online at your local library.

Finding reliable critical essays on individual authors or works of American literature can be more challenging. Cambridge University Press has recently initiated a new series of books devoted to major authors and intended to appeal to general readers. These Cambridge Introductions treat such authors as T. S. Eliot, William Faulkner, F. Scott Fitzgerald, Nathaniel Hawthorne, Herman Melville, Ezra Pound, and Mark Twain. The volumes in the more established Cambridge Companions series are more detailed. Exemplary titles in this series discuss Edward Albee, Willa Cather, Ralph Ellison, Robert Frost, Ernest Hemingway, Henry James, Arthur Miller, Eugene

O'Neill, Sylvia Plath, Edgar Allan Poe, Henry David Thoreau, Edith Wharton, Walt Whitman, and Tennessee Williams.

For decades, Oxford University Press has published the *Oxford Companion to American Literature* (1941; 6th ed., 1995), an encyclopedic work that provides brief biographies and plot summaries of many authors and works. Jay Parini's four-volume *Oxford Encyclopedia of American Literature* (Oxford University Press, 2004) contains much fuller information than the *Companion*. Recently the press has expanded its Oxford Handbooks series to include topics in American literature. The first volume, *The Oxford Handbook to Early American Literature*, appeared in 2008. It consists of more than two dozen lengthy essays by different contributors devoted to various aspects of American literature through the eighteenth century. The work constitutes the fullest collaborative history of early American literature available. By the time the series is complete, it will cover the entire history of American literature.

Other useful references works include *The Continuum Encyclopedia of American Literature* (Continuum, 2005), edited by Steven Serafin and Alfred Bendixen; *American History Through Literature, 1820–1870* (Scribner, 2006), a three-volume work edited by Janet Gabler-Hover and Robert Sattelmeyer; and *American History Through Literature, 1870–1920* (Scribner, 2006), a three-volume work edited by Tom Quirk and Gary Scharnhorst. Author interviews can also be a useful source of information. The Literary Conversations series published by the University Press of Mississippi is generally excellent.

Chapter 1

Kevin J. Hayes, *Cambridge Introduction to Herman Melville* (Cambridge University Press, 2007).

Terence Martin, "The Negative Structures of American Literature," *American Literature* 57 (1985): 1–22.

William McKeen, *Outlaw Journalist: The Life and Times of Hunter S. Thompson* (Norton, 2008).

Edwin Haviland Miller, *Walt Whitman's "Song of Myself": A Mosaic of Interpretations* (University of Iowa Press, 1989).

Arnold Rampersad, *Ralph Ellison: A Biography* (Knopf, 2007).

Robert D. Richardson, *Emerson, the Mind on Fire: A Biography* (University of California Press, 1995).

Geoffrey Sanborn, "A Confused Beginning: *The Narrative of Arthur Gordon Pym, of Nantucket*," in *Cambridge Companion to Edgar Allan Poe*, ed. Kevin J. Hayes (Cambridge University Press, 2002), 163–77.

Karen Schramm, "Promotion Literature," in *Oxford Handbook of Early American Literature*, ed. Kevin J. Hayes (Oxford University Press, 2008), 69–89.

Terry Southern, *Now Dig This: The Unspeakable Writings of Terry Southern, 1950–1995*, ed. Nile Southern and Josh Alan Friedman (Grove, 2001).

Jean Fagan Yellin, *Harriet Jacobs: A Life* (Basic Civitas Books, 2004).

Chapter 2

Percy G. Adams, *Travelers and Travel Liars, 1660–1800* (University of California Press, 1962).

Kevin J. Hayes, *An American Cycling Odyssey, 1887* (University of Nebraska Press, 2002).

Paul Horgan, *Josiah Gregg and His Vision of the Early West* (Farrar Straus Giroux, 1979).

Robert Micklus, *The Comic Genius of Dr. Alexander Hamilton* (University of Tennessee Press, 1990).

Daniel Royot, "Picaresque Travel Narratives," in *Oxford Handbook of Early American Literature*, ed. Kevin J. Hayes (Oxford University Press, 2008), 215–38.

Thomas P. Slaughter, *The Natures of John and William Bartram* (Knopf, 1996).

Jennifer Speake (ed.), *Literature of Travel and Exploration: An Encyclopedia*, 3 vols. (Fitzroy Dearborn, 2003).

Donald Worster, *A River Running West: The Life of John Wesley Powell* (Oxford University Press, 2000).

Chapter 3

Vincent Carretta, *Equiano, the African: Biography of a Self-Made Man* (University of Georgia Press, 2005).

Lorrayne Carroll, "Captivity Literature," in *Oxford Handbook of Early American Literature*, ed. Kevin J. Hayes (Oxford University Press, 2008), 143–68.

Holly E. Farrington, "Narrating the Jazz Life: Three Approaches to Jazz Autobiography," *Popular Music and Society* 29 (2006): 375–86.

Jürgen E. Grandt, *Kinds of Blue: The Jazz Aesthetic in African American Narrative* (Ohio State University Press, 2004).

Christopher Harlos, "Jazz Autobiography: Theory, Practice, Politics," in *Representing Jazz*, ed. Krin Gabbard (Duke University Press, 1995), 131–66.

J. A. Leo Lemay, *Life of Benjamin Franklin*, 3 vols. (University of Pennsylvania Press, 2006–8).

Hyun Yi Kang (ed.), *Writing Self, Writing Nation: A Collection of Essays on Dictee by Theresa Hak Kyung Cha* (Third Woman Press, 1994).

William S. McFeely, *Frederick Douglass* (Norton, 1991).

Chapter 4

Paula Blanchard, *Sarah Orne Jewett: Her World and Her Work* (Addison-Wesley, 1994).

Robert H. Brinkmeyer, *The Art and Vision of Flannery O'Connor* (Louisiana State University Press, 1989).

Kevin J. Hayes (ed.), *Cambridge Companion to Edgar Allan Poe* (Cambridge University Press, 2002).

———, *Stephen Crane* (Northcote House, 2004).

James H. Justus, *Fetching the Old Southwest: Humorous Writing from Longstreet to Twain* (University of Missouri Press, 2004).

Edwin Haviland Miller, *Salem Is My Dwelling Place: A Life of Nathaniel Hawthorne* (University of Iowa Press, 1991).

Joyce Carol Oates (ed.), *The Oxford Book of American Short Stories* (Oxford University Press, 1992).

Ron Powers, *Mark Twain: A Life* (Free Press, 2005).

Jeanne Campbell Reesman, *Jack London: A Study of the Short Fiction* (Twayne, 1999).

Hazel Rowley, *Richard Wright: The Life and Times* (Henry Holt, 2001).

Chapter 5

Milton J. Bates, *Wallace Stevens: A Mythology of Self* (University of California Press, 1985).

Chris Beyers, "Augustan American Verse," in *Oxford Handbook to Early American Literature*, ed. Kevin J. Hayes (Oxford University Press, 2008), 189–214.

Ronald A. Bosco and Jillmarie Murphy, "New England Poetry," in *Oxford Handbook to Early American Literature*, ed. Kevin J. Hayes (Oxford University Press, 2008), 115–41.

Humphrey Carpenter, *A Serious Character: The Life of Ezra Pound* (Houghton Mifflin, 1988).

Kevin J. Hayes, *Poe and the Printed Word* (Cambridge University Press, 2000).

Daniel Hoffman, *Poetry of Stephen Crane* (Columbia University Press, 1957).

J. A. Leo Lemay, *Calendar of American Poetry in the Colonial Newspapers and Magazines and in the Major English Magazines Through 1765* (American Antiquarian Society, 1972).

———, "Southern Colonial Grotesque: Robert Bolling's 'Neanthe.'" *Mississippi Quarterly* 35 (1982): 97–126.

Jay Leyda, *Years and Hours of Emily Dickinson* (Yale University Press, 1960).

Jerome Loving, *Walt Whitman: The Song of Himself* (University of California Press, 1999).

Hershel Parker, *Melville: The Making of the Poet* (Northwestern University Press, 2008).

David Perkins, *A History of Modern Poetry*, 2 vols. (Belknap Press of Harvard University Press, 1976–87).

Anne Stevenson, *Bitter Fame: A Life of Sylvia Plath* (Houghton Mifflin, 1989).

Colin Wells, "Revolutionary Verse," in *Oxford Handbook to Early American Literature*, ed. Kevin J. Hayes (Oxford University Press, 2008), 505–24.

Chapter 6

Stephen A. Black, *Eugene O'Neill: Beyond Mourning and Tragedy* (Yale University Press, 1999).

Shaun Considine, *Mad as Hell: The Life and Work of Paddy Chayefsky* (Random House, 1994).

Martin Gottfried, *Arthur Miller: His Life and Work* (Da Capo, 2003).

Kevin J. Hayes (ed.), *Sam Peckinpah: Interviews* (University Press of Mississippi, 2008).

Winifred Morgan, *An American Icon: Brother Jonathan and American Identity* (University of Delaware Press, 1988).

Donald Spoto, *The Kindness of Strangers: The Life of Tennessee Williams* (Little, Brown, 1985).

Tom Stempel, *Storytellers to the Nation: A History of American Television Writing* (Continuum, 1992).

Chapter 7

Louis Auchincloss, *Reading Henry James* (University of Minnesota Press, 1975).

Susan Goodman, *Edith Wharton's Inner Circle* (University of Texas Press, 1994).

Kevin J. Hayes (ed.), *Conversations with Jack Kerouac* (University Press of Mississippi, 2005).

William Marling, *American Roman Noir: Hammett, Cain, and Chandler* (University of Georgia Press, 1995).

Jay Parini, *One Matchless Time: A Life of William Faulkner* (HarperCollins, 2004).

Jean Pfaelzer, *Rebecca Harding Davis and the Origins of American Social Realism* (University of Pittsburgh Press, 1996).

Kate Phillips, *Helen Hunt Jackson: A Literary Life* (University of California Press, 2003).

Carol J. Singley, *Edith Wharton: Matters of Mind and Spirit* (Cambridge University Press, 1995).

Laura E. Skandera-Trombley, *Critical Essays on Maxine Hong Kingston* (G. K. Hall, 1998).

Adam J. Sorkin (ed.), *Conversations with Joseph Heller* (University Press of Mississippi, 1993).

Andrew Turnbull, *Scott Fitzgerald* (1962; reprinted, Grove Press, 2001).

Marc Weingarten, *The Gang That Wouldn't Write Straight: Wolfe, Thompson, Didion, and the New Journalism Revolution* (Crown, 2006).

Chapter 8

Valerie Boyd, *Wrapped in Rainbows: The Life of Zora Neale Hurston* (Scribner, 2003).

Elizabeth Bishop, *One Art: Letters*, ed. Robert Giroux (Farrar, Straus, Giroux, 1994).

Kevin J. Hayes, *Edgar Allan Poe* (Reaktion, 2009).

———(ed.), *Henry James: The Contemporary Reviews* (Cambridge University Press, 1996).

Cary Nelson and Ed Folsom, *W. S. Merwin: Essays on the Poetry* (University of Illinois Press, 1987).

Hershel Parker, *Herman Melville: A Biography*, 2 vols. (Johns Hopkins University Press, 1996–2002).

Russell Reising, *Loose Ends: Closure and Crisis in the American Social Text* (Duke University Press, 1996).

INDEX

Organized primarily by name, this index lists the people mentioned in the text and also provides their birth and death dates. Furthermore, it identifies them by their professions or the roles in which they excelled as writers. Figures outside the history of American literature are also identified by nationality. Titles of individual literary works are listed under authors' names. In short, this index has been organized not only as a guide to the present work, but also as a mini-biographical dictionary.

INDEX